Climbing Everest

The Complete Writings

of

GEORGE LEIGH MALLORY

Peter Gillman
Introduction

GIBSON SQUARE

This edition published in 2023 in the USA by Gibson Square

US +1 646 216 9488

rights@gibsonsquare.com
www.gibsonsquare.com

Papers used by Gibson Square are natural, recyclable products made from wood grown in sustainable forests; inks used are vegetable based. Manufacturing conforms to ISO 14001, and is accredited to FSC and PEFC chain of custody schemes. Colour-printing is through a certified CarbonNeutral® company that offsets its CO_2 emissions.

CONTENTS

CONTENTS

INTRODUCTION
Peter Gillman

On 12 April 1922, George Mallory sat down to write a letter to his wife Ruth. The British Everest expedition had just reached the Tibetan fortress town of Kampa Dzong, having fought its way through a blizzard which had obliterated their tracks and rendered the Tibetan plateau into a wasteland of snow and ice. As Mallory related, he was wearing two sets of underclothes—one wool, the other silk—a flannel shirt, a sleeved waistcoat, a lambskin jacket and a Burberry coat, as well as plus fours, two pairs of woollen stockings, and a pair of sheepskin boots. Yet his hands were so cold, he told Ruth, that he could hardly manage to grip his pen.

It says a great deal about Mallory's tenacity and dedication that he completed his letter, telling Ruth about 'the shadows of mountains moving over the plains' and the 'delicate shades of red and yellow and brown' of the landscape before the snow came. It also reveals much about Mallory's view of himself as writer. In the first place, he regarded it his duty to posterity that he should faithfully record the sights and events the 1922 expedition encountered on its arduous five-week trek to Everest. In the days when history was still inscribed in pen and ink, letters were seen as vital links in the testimonial chain, and Mallory certainly had a sense of the expedition's part in the developing saga of human exploration.

His writing also met more personal goals. George and Ruth Mallory had married in July 1914, on the very eve of the First World War. As an artillery officer, Mallory spent a year and a half, with intervals, on the western front. Throughout that period he and Ruth had sustained their marriage by writing to each other regularly—in Ruth's case, every single day. Thus when Mallory departed for Everest, doing so three times in the space of four years, they continued the practice as a way of keeping their relationship and their love alive.

Both during the war, and while Mallory was away on Everest, their exchanges were always endearingly intimate: Ruth tells George about the latest doings—and misdeeds—of their three young children, Clare, Berry and John. She recites her domestic concerns, her encounters with George's parents and with hers, the state of the garden at their home in Godalming, Surrey. George is almost as gossipy in response, giving his views of his brother officers on the Western Front and his fellow climbers in Tibet, as well as describing the more momentous progress of both the war in the France and the expedition in Tibet. Their letters are all the more poignant given that their love was doomed, destined to end when Mallory disappeared near the summit of Everest a little less than ten years after they were married.

Once back home in Godalming, Mallory—to use a very modern phrase—recycled his letters to provide his contributions to the official books of the expeditions. Although he removed the less discreet references to his fellow-climbers, the thrust of the narrative, and the quality of his descriptions, are essentially the same. The account which constitutes six chapters of *Everest Reconnaissance 1921* shines even more by contrast with the eleven flat, tedious chapters written by Lt Col Charles Howard-Bury, the expedition leader, which Mallory justly described as 'quite dreadfully bad'.

It was in response to this kind of monotonous prose, devoid of all affect, that Mallory had been developing his own theories of writing. It also stemmed from his involvement with the Bloomsbury group and what was termed the Cambridge School of Friendship, where emotional openness and honesty were all. Mallory believed it was vital that mountaineering writing should function on an emotional level, disclosing the participants' feelings and attempting to evoke them in the reader. Not for him the stiff upper lip of traditional mountaineering prose, whose authors did their best to conceal their sentiments behind layers of irony and understatement.

Mallory liked to conjure new epithets too: at the tiny settlement of Shilling during the approach march in 1921, he wrote how the wind, a relentless, ever-present force, swept over the sand of a river bank so that it rippled like a sea of watered silk. Such descriptive touches illustrate Mallory's primary delight in savouring new experiences, one of the key motivations of his life, and his determination to render them in a way that others—starting with his beloved Ruth—could comprehend.

Mallory had embarked on this process at least a decade before. His published canon is not large: he wrote a total of six articles for the two principal climbing publications of the day: the *Alpine Journal*, published by the Alpine Club, and the *Climbers Club Journal*. The first of these, *The Mountaineer as Artist*, written in 1913, illuminates his theories about both mountaineering literature and writing in general.

Mallory's immediate topic was the meaning of risk in mountaineering. It is significant that he should address this, as mountaineering's practitioners can attempt to delude themselves—and family and friends—into believing that theirs is not an unduly dangerous pursuit, providing only that they obey the safety rules. Equally telling, Mallory wrote his article at a time when the select coterie who comprised the core of British mountaineering were reeling from the deaths of several of their members in climbing accidents in Snowdonia and the Alps.

Geoffrey Winthrop Young, one of the impresarios of the British climbing world, and the principal sponsor of Mallory's career, was among the most distressed at the deaths, observing that they marked the end of climbing's age of innocence. Mallory courageously grappled with these issues in the article, scrutinising the validity of the climbers' experiences, and producing the metaphor of a symphony to represent the rhythms of climbing's aesthetic and emotional appeal. Although Mallory was uncertain whether his article had succeeded in its aim, it represented a prescient attempt to identify the emotional core of all sporting experiences which prefigures the recent wave of sports writing.

Mallory resumed these explorations in his second article, 'Mont Blanc from the Col du Géant by the Eastern Buttress of Mont Maudit', written in 1917 while he was away from the front at an army training camp in Winchester. Mallory had observed that the terminology of conflict and war was habitually deployed to create an antagonism between mountaineer and mountain. His article describes an ascent of Mont Maudit and its neighbour Mont Blanc which he had undertaken with two friends in 1911. This time he portrays the climb as an inner journey, mediating his actions through his emotional responses to the sequence of events, from his guilt at kicking over the breakfast stove, to his alarm over the most dangerous section of the climb. Then, at the summit, Mallory rejects the notions of victory and conquest. In the most-quoted passage of his writing, he wrote: 'We're not exultant; but delighted, joyful; soberly astonished....Have we vanquished an enemy? Not but ourselves....'

It was not long afterwards that Mallory attempted to forge a career based in part on his writing. He had been a teacher at Charterhouse School in Godalming but resigned to join the first British Everest expedition, the 1921 reconnaissance on which Mallory was to play the key role in identifying the potential route to the summit from the north. His plan was to make a living from writing and lecturing about both his exploits on Everest and broader topics, such as entry for an encyclopaedia about the Himalayas, and his article for the US-published *Asia* magazine in 1923. Sadly, he did not make the income he had hoped, and in autumn 1923 he and his family moved to Cambridge, where he took up a post as an extra-mural lecturer in history.

It is a terrible irony that one reason he was compelled to renounce his career as a writer was the parsimony of the Mount Everest Committee, which organised the three expeditions in which Mallory took part. When Mallory provided his chapters for the account of the 1921 reconnaissance, he did so on the clear under-standing that he would be paid for his work. By November 1923, just three months before he departed on his third and final expedi-tion, Mallory had still not been paid. But when he pressed the com-mittee he received a dusty answer. The committee revoked the pre-vious undertaking and told Mallory no payment would be forth-coming—while sanctimoniously adding that it 'fully appreciated the value of your contributions'.

Whether the committee did appreciate the quality of Mallory's contribution is far from clear, since it was so radically different from the turgid account by Howard-Bury, the reconnaissance leader. It represents the best of Mallory's writings, a pacy narrative, com-posed in the form of a quest, that occupies a mid-point between his experimental writing and his more pragmatic journalism. It is all the more remarkable for capturing the sense in which the 1921 recon-naissance was a venture into the unknown. No westerner had been within 60 miles of Everest, nor did it appear on any detailed maps. For much of the trek through Tibet the expedition was unable to see the mountain as it was obscured by clouds.

As both adventurer and writer, Mallory was waiting for Everest to come into view. He wanted there to be a moment of revelation, providing him with a construct to counterpoint the frustration he and his companions had experienced to that juncture. On 12 June he and his partner Guy Bullock climbed a hill above the Yaru river and looked in the direction of where Everest should be. Over the next hour the clouds gradually parted, at first giving fragmentary glimpses of glaciers and ridges, until the mountain's great north face and its summit pyramid were finally revealed.

He described the unveiling of this vision in a letter to Ruth on 15 June, which he reworked when he came to write his chapters for the expedition book. He also deployed a simile which was central to his motivations and his life. 'Mountain shapes are often fantastic seen through a mist,' Mallory wrote; 'these were like the wildest creation of a dream.'

The notion of the dream occurs in several of Mallory's previous letters and articles, but here achieves its greatest force. The drive to fulfil his dreams inspired Mallory's decisions and actions, and provides a key to understanding both him and his colleagues in their venture into the unknown. In their willingness to confront the dangers that lay ahead, they serve as a testament to the optimism and defiance that are at the core of human nature.

There is a small postscript I should like to offer. In 2000, the biography of George Mallory, *The Wildest Dream*, written by myself and my wife Leni, was published. We were delighted and flattered by its reception, above all when it was awarded the Boardman Tasker prize for Mountain Writing. We were soon convinced that there was a second book to be published—the collected writings of our protagonist and hero. What ensued is the familiar and wearying tale of attempting to find a publisher who shared our belief. We were turned down three times and then moved on to another project. It was thus with delight, tinged with envy, that we learned that Gibson Square Books was publishing this collection of Mallory's writing. We trust and hope that its readers will share our view of the qualities of George Mallory, bold, innovative, and inspirational in his writing as in his life.

Climbing Everest

'From Everest we expect no mercy.'
George Leigh Mallory

1

THE MOUNTAINEER AS ARTIST

I seem to distinguish two sorts of climber, those who take a high line about climbing and those who take no particular line at all. It is depressing to think how little I understand either, and I can hardly believe that the second sort are such fools as I imagine. Perhaps the distinction has no reality; it may be that it is only a question of attitude. Still, even as an attitude, the position of the first sort of climber strikes a less violent shock of discord with mere reason. Climbing for them means something more than a common amusement, and more than other forms of athletic pursuit mean to other men; it has a recognised importance in life. If you could deprive them of it they would be conscious of a definite degradation, a loss of virtue. For those who take the high line about it climbing may be one of the modern ways of salvation along with slumming, statistics, and other forms of culture, and more complete than any of these. They have an arrogance with regard to this hobby never equalled even by a little king among grouse-killers. It never, for instance, presents itself to them as comparable with field sports. They assume an unmeasured superiority. And yet—they give no explanation.

I am myself one of the arrogant sort, and may serve well for example, because I happen also to be a sportsman. It is not intended that any inference as to my habits should follow from this premise. You may easily be a sportsman though you have never walked with a gun under your arm nor bestride a tall horse in your pink. I am a sportsman simply because men say that I am; it would be impossible to convince them of the contrary, and it's no use complaining; and, once I have humbly accepted my fate and settled down in this way of life, I am proud to show, if I can, how I deserve the title. Though a sportsman may be guiltless of sporting deeds, one who has acquired the sporting reputation will show cause in kind if he may. Now, it is abundantly clear that any expedition on the high Alps is of a sporting nature; it is almost aggressively sporting. And yet it would never occur to me to prove my title by any reference to mountaineering in the Alps, nor would it occur to any other climber of the arrogant sort who may also be a sportsman. We set climbing on a pedestal above the common recreations of men. We hold it apart and label it as something that has a special value.

This, though it passes with all too little comment, is a plain act of rebellion. It is a serious deviation from the normal standard of rightness and wrongness, and if we were to succeed in establishing our value for mountaineering we should upset the whole order of society, just as completely as it would be upset if a sufficient number of people who claimed to be enlightened were to eat eggs with knives and regard with disdain the poor folk who ate them with spoons.

But there is a propriety of behaviour for rebels as for others. Society can at least expect of rebels that they explain themselves. Other men are exempt from this duty because they use the recognised labels in the conventional ways. Sporting practice and religious observance were at one time placed above, or below, the need of explanation. They were bottled and labelled 'Extra dry,' and this valuation was accepted as a premise for a priori judgments by society in general. Rebel minorities have sometimes behaved in the same way, and by the very arrogance of their dogmatism have made a rev-olution. The porridge-with-salt men have introduced a fashion which decrees that it is right to eat salt with porridge, and no less wrong to conceal its true nature by any other disguise than to pass the bottle from left to right instead of opposite-wise. This triumph was secured only by self-assured arrogance. But the correct method for rebels is that they set forth their case for the world to see.

Climbers who, like myself, take the high line have much to explain, and it is time they set about it. Notoriously they endanger their lives. With what object? If only for some physical pleasure, to enjoy certain movements of the body and to experience the zest of emulation, then it is not worth while. Climbers are only a particu-larly foolish set of desperadoes; they are on the same plane with hunters, and many degrees less reasonable. The only defence for mountaineering puts it on a higher plane than mere physical sensa-tion. It is asserted that the climber experiences higher emotions; he gets some good for his soul. His opponent may well feel sceptical about this argument. He, too, may claim to consider his soul's good when he can take a holiday. Probably it is true of anyone who spends a well-earned fortnight in healthy enjoyment at the seaside that he comes back a better, that is to say a more virtuous mart than he went. How are the climber's joys worth more than the seaside? What are these higher emotions to which he refers so elusively? And if they really are so valuable, is there no safer way of reaching them? Do mountaineers consider these questions and answer them again and again from fresh experience, or are they content with some magic certainty born of comparative ignorance long ago?

It would be a wholesome tonic, perhaps, more often to meet an adversary who argued on these lines. In practice I find that few men ever want to discuss mountaineering seriously. I suppose they imag-ine that a discussion with me would be unprofitable; and I must confess that if anyone does open the question my impulse is to put him off. I can assume a vague disdain for civilisation, and I can make phrases about beautiful surroundings, and puff them out, as one who has a secret and does not care to reveal it because no one would understand—phrases which refer to the divine riot of Nature in her ecstasy of making mountains.

Thus I appeal to the effect of mountain scenery upon my aesthetic sensibility. But, even if I can communicate by words a true feeling, I have explained nothing. Aesthetic delight is vitally connected with our performance, but it neither explains nor excuses it. No one for a moment dreams that our apparently wilful proceedings are determined merely by our desire to see what is beautiful. The mountain railway could cater for such desires. By providing view-points at a number of stations, and by concealing all signs of its own mechanism, it might be so completely organised that all the aesthetic joys of the mountaineer should be offered to its intrepid ticket-holders. It would achieve this object with a comparatively small expenditure of time, and would even have, one might suppose, a decisive advantage by affording to all lovers of the mountains the opportunity of sharing their emotions with a large and varied multitude of their fellow-men. And yet the idea of associating this mechanism with a snow mountain is the abomination of every species of mountaineer. To him it appears as a kind of rape. The fact that he so regards it indicates the emphasis with which he rejects the crude aesthetic reasons as his central defence.

I suppose that, in the opinion of many people who have opportunities of judging, mountaineers have no ground for claiming for their pursuit a superiority as regards the natural beauties that attend it. And certainly many huntsmen would resent their making any such claim. We cannot, therefore, remove mountaineering from the plane of hunting by a composite representation of its merits—by asserting that physical and aesthetic joys are blended for us and not for others.

Nevertheless, I am still arrogant, and still confident in the superiority of mountaineering over all other forms of recreation. But what do I mean by this superiority? And in what measure do I claim it? On what level do we place mountaineering? What place in the whole order of experience is occupied by our experience as mountaineers? The answer to these questions must be very nearly connected with the whole explanation of our position; it may actually be found to include in itself a defence of mountaineering.

It must be admitted at the outset that our periodic literature gives little indication that our performance is concerned no less with the spiritual side of us than with the physical. This is, in part, because we require certain practical information of anyone who describes an expedition. Our journals, with one exception, do not pretend to be elevated literature, but aim only at providing useful knowledge for climbers. With this purpose we try to show exactly where upon a mountain our course lay, in what manner the conditions of snow and ice and rocks and weather were or were not favourable to our enterprise, and what were the actual difficulties we had to overcome and the dangers we had to meet. Naturally, if we accept these circumstances, the impulse for literary expression vanishes; not so much because the matter is not suitable as because, for literary expression, it is too difficult to handle. A big expedition in the Alps, say a traverse of Mont Blanc, would be a superb theme for an epic poem. But we are not all even poets, still less Homers or Miltons. We do, indeed, possess lyric poetry that is concerned with mountains, and value it highly for the expression of much that we feel about them. But little of it can be said to suggest that mountaineering in the technical sense offers an emotional experience which cannot otherwise be reached. A few essays and a few descriptions do give some indication that the spiritual part of man is concerned. Most of those who describe expeditions do not even treat them as adventure, still less as being connected with any emotional experience peculiar to mountaineering. Some writers, after the regular careful references to matters of plain fact, insert a paragraph dealing summarily with an aesthetic experience; the greater part make a bare allusion to such feelings or neglect them altogether, and perhaps these are the wisest sort.

And yet it is not so very difficult to write about aesthetic impressions in some way so as to give pleasure. If we do not ask too much, many writers are able to please us in this respect. We may be pleased, without being stirred to the depths, by anyone who can make us believe that he has experienced aesthetically; we may not be able to feel with him what he has felt, but if he talks about it simply we may be quite delighted to perceive that he has felt as we too are capable of feeling. Mountaineers who write do not, as a rule, succeed even in this small degree. If they are so bold as to attempt a sunset or sunrise, we too often feel uncertain as we read that they have felt anything—and this even though we may know quite well that they are accustomed to feel as we feel ourselves.

These observations about our mountain literature are not made by way of censure or in disappointment; they are put forward as phenomena, which have to be explained, not so much by the nature of mountaineers, but rather by the nature of their performance. The explanation which commends itself to me is derived very simply from the conception of mountaineering, which, expressed or unexpressed, is common, I imagine, to all us of the arrogant sort. We do not think that our aesthetic experiences of sunrises and sunsets and clouds and thunder are supremely important facts in mountaineering, but rather that they cannot thus be separated and catalogued and described individually as experiences at all. They are not incidental in mountaineering, but a vital and inseparable part of it; they are not ornamental, but structural; they are not various items causing emotion but parts of an emotional whole; they are the crystal pools perhaps, but they owe their life to a continuous stream.

It is this unity that makes so many attempts to describe aesthetic detail seem futile. Somehow they miss the point and fail to touch us. It is because they are only fragments. If we take one moment and present its emotional quality apart from the whole, it has lost the very essence that gave it a value. If we write about an expedition from the emotional point of view in any part of it, we ought so to write about the whole adventure from beginning to end.

A day well spent in the Alps is like some great symphony. Andante, andantissimo sometimes, is the first movement—the grim, sickening plod up the moraine. But how forgotten when the blue light of dawn flickers over the hard, clean snow! The new *motif* is ushered in, as it were, very gently on the lesser wind instruments, hautbois and flutes, remote but melodious and infinitely hopeful, caught by the violins in the growing light, and torn out by all the bows with quivering chords as the summits, one by one, are enmeshed in the gold web of day, till at last the whole band, in triumphant accord, has seized the air and romps in magnificent frolic, because there you are at last marching, all a-tingle with warm blood, under the sun. And so throughout the day successive moods induce the symphonic whole—allegro while you break the back of an expedition and the issue is still in doubt; scherzo, perhaps, as you leap tip the final rocks of the arête or cut steps in a last short slope, with the ice-chips dancing and swimming and bubbling and bounding with magic gaiety over the crisp surface in their mad glissade; and then, for the descent, sometimes again andante, because, while the summit was still to win, you forgot that the business of descending may be serious and long; but in the end scherzo once more—with the brakes on for sunset.

Expeditions in the Alps are all different, no less than symphonies are different, and each is a fresh experience. Not all are equally buoyant with hope and strength; nor is it only the proportion of grim to pleasant that varies, but no less the quality of these and other ingredients and the manner of their mixing. But every mountain adventure is emotionally complete. The spirit goes on a journey just as does the body, and this journey has a beginning and an end, and is concerned with all that happens between these extremities.

You cannot say that one part of your adventure was emotional while another was not, any more than you can say of your journey that one part was travelling and another was not. You cannot subtract parts and still have the whole. Each part depends for its value upon all the other parts, and the manner in which it is related to them. The glory of sunrise in the Alps is not independent of what has passed and what's to come; without the day that is dying and the night that is to come the reverie of sunset would be less suggestive, and the deep valley-lights would lose their promise of repose. Still more, the ecstasy of the summit is conditioned by the events of getting up and the prospects of getting down.

Mountain scenes occupy the same place in our consciousness with remembered melody. It is all one whether I find myself humming the air of some great symphonic movement or gazing upon some particular configuration of rock and snow, or peak and glacier, or even more humbly upon some colour harmony of meadow and sweet pinewood in Alpine valley. Impressions of things seen return unbidden to the mind, so that we seem to have whole series of places where we love to spend idle moments, inns, as it were, inviting us by the roadside, and many of them pleasant and comfortable Gorphwysfas, so well known to us by now that we make the journey easily enough with a homing instinct, and never feel a shock of surprise, however remote they seem, when we find ourselves there. Many people, it appears, have strange dreamlands, where they are accustomed to wander at ease, where no 'dull brain perplexes and retards,' nor tired body and heavy limbs, but where the whole emotional being flows, unrestrained and unencumbered, it knows not whither, like a stream rippling happily in its clean sandy bed, careless towards the infinite. My own experience has more of the earth. My mental homes are real places, distinctly seen and not hard to recognise. Only a little while ago, when a sentence I was writing got into a terrible tangle, I visited one of them. An infant river meanders coolly in a broad, grassy valley; it winds along as gently almost as some glassy snake of the plains, for the valley is so flat that its slope is imperceptible. The green hills on either side are smooth and pleasing to the eye, and eventually close in, though not completely. Here the stream plunges down a steep and craggy hillside far into the shadow of a deeper valley. You may follow it down by a rough path, and then, turning aside, before you quite reach the bottom of the second valley, along a grassy ledge, you may find a modest inn. The scene was visited in reality by three tired walkers at the end of a first day in the Alps a few seasons back. It is highly agreeable. When I discover myself looking again upon the features of this landscape, I walk no longer in a vain shadow, disquieting myself, but a delicious serenity embraces my whole being. In another scene which I still sometimes visit, though not so often as formerly, the main feature is a number of uniform truncated cones with a circular base of, perhaps, 8 inches diameter; they are made of reddish sand. They were, in fact, made long ago by filling a flower-pot with sandy soil from the country garden where I spent a considerable part of my childhood. The emotional quality of this scene is more exciting than that of the other. It recalls the first occasion upon which I made sand-pies, and something of the creative force of that moment is associated with the tidy little heaps of reddish sand.

For any ardent mountaineer whose imaginative parts are made like mine, normally, as I should say, the mountains will naturally supply a large part of this hinterland, and the more important scenes will probably be mountainous—an indication in itself that the mountain experiences, unless they are merely terrible, are particularly valuable.

It is difficult to see why certain moments should have this queer vitality, as though the mind's home contained some mystic cavern set with gems which wait only for a gleam of light to reveal their hidden glory. What principle is it that determines this vitality? Perhaps the analogy with musical experience may still suffice. Mountain scenes appear to recur, not only in the same quality with tunes from a great work, say, Mozart or Beethoven, but from the same differentiating cause. It is not mere intensity of feeling that determines the places of tunes in my subconscious self, but chiefly some other principle. When the chords of melody are split, and unsatisfied suggestions of complete harmony are tossed among the instruments; when the firm rhythm is lost in remote pools and eddies, the mind roams perplexed; it experiences remorse and associates it with no cause; grief, and it names no sad event; desires crying aloud and unfulfilled, and yet it will not formulate the object of them; but when the great tide of music rises with a resolved purpose, floating the strewn wreckage and bearing it up together in its embracing stream, like a supreme spirit in the glorious act of creation, then the vague distresses and cravings are satisfied, a divine completeness of harmony possesses all the senses and the mind as though the universe and the individual were in exact accord, pursuing a common aim with the efficiency of mechanical perfection. Similarly, some parts of a climbing day give us the feeling of things unfulfilled; we doubt and tremble; we go forward not as men determined to reach a fixed goal; our plans do not convince us and miscarry; discomforts are not willingly accepted as a proper necessity; spirit and body seem to betray each other: but a time comes when all this is changed and we experience a harmony and a satisfaction. The individual is in a sense submerged, yet not so as to be less conscious; rather his consciousness is specially alert, and he comes to a finer realisation of himself than ever before. It is these moments of supremely harmonious experience that remain always with us and part of us. Other times and other scenes besides may be summoned back to gleam across the path, elusive revenants; but those that are born of the supreme accord are more substantial; they are the real immortals. Sensation may fill the mind with melody remembered, so that the great leading airs of a symphony become an emotional commonplace for all who have heard it, and for mountaineers it may with no less facility evoke a mountain scene.

But once again. What is the value of our emotional experience among mountains? We may show by comparison the kind of feeling we have, but might not that comparison be applied with a similar result in other spheres?

How it would disturb the cool contempt of the arrogant mountaineer to whisper in his ear, 'Why not drop it and take up, say, Association football?' Not, of course, if a footballer made the remark, because the mountaineer would merely humour him as he would humour a child. That, at least, is the line I should take myself, and I can't imagine that, for instance, a proper president of the Alpine Club, if approached in this way by the corresponding functionary of the A.F.A., could adopt any other. But supposing a member of the club were to make the suggestion—with the emendation, lest this should be ridiculous, of golf instead of football—imagine the righteousness of his wrath and the majesty of his anger! And yet it is as well to consider whether the footballers, golfers, etc., of this world have not some experience akin to ours. The exteriors of sportsmen are so arranged as to suggest that they have not; but if we are to pursue the truth in a whole-hearted fashion we must, at all costs, go further and see what lies beyond the faces and clothes of sporting men. Happily, as a sportsman myself, I know what the real feelings of sportsmen are; it is clear enough to me that the great majority of them have the same sort of experience as mountaineers.

It is abundantly clear to me, and even too abundantly. The fact that sportsmen are, with regard to their sport, highly emotional beings is at once so strange and so true that a lifetime might well be spent in the testing of it. Very pleasant it would be to linger among the curious jargons, the outlandish manners—barbaric heartiness, mediaeval chivalry, 'side' and 'swank,' if these can be distinguished, in their various appearances—and the mere facial expressions of the different species in the genus; and to see how all alike have one main object, to disguise the depth of their real sentiment. But these matters are to be enjoyed and digested in the plenty of leisure hours, and I must put them by for now. The plain facts are sufficient for this occasion. The elation of sportsmen in success, their depression in failure, their long-spun vivacity in anecdote—these are the great tests, and by their quality may be seen the elemental play of emotions among all kinds of sportsmen. The footballers, the cricketers, the golfers, the batters and ballers—to be short, of all the one hundred and thirty-one varieties, all dream by day and by night as the climber dreams. Spheroidic prodigies are immortal each in its locality. The place comes back to the hero with the culminating event the moment when a round, inanimate object was struck supremely well; and all the great race of hunters, in more lands than one, the men who hunt fishes and fowls and beasts after their kind, from perch to spotted sea-serpent, fat pheasant to dainty lark or thrush, tame deer to jungle-bred monster, all hunters dream of killing animals, whether they be small or great, and whether they be gentle or ferocious. Sport is for sportsmen a part of their emotional experience, as mountaineering is for mountaineers.

How, then, shall we distinguish emotionally between the mountaineer and the sportsman?

The great majority of men are in a sense artists; some are active and creative, and some participate passively. No doubt those who create differ in some way fundamentally from those who do not create; but they hold this artistic impulse in common: all alike desire expression for the emotional side of their nature. The behaviour of those who are devoted to the higher forms of Art shows this clearly enough. It is clearest of all, perhaps, in the drama, in dancing, and in music. Not only those who perform are artists, but also those who are moved by the performance. Artists, in this sense, are not distinguished by the power of expressing emotion, but the power of feeling that emotional experience out of which Art is made. We recognise this when we speak of individuals as artistic, though they have no pretension to create Art. Arrogant mountaineers are all artistic, independently of any other consideration, because they cultivate emotional experience for its own sake; and so for the same reason are sportsmen. It is not paradoxical to assert that all sportsmen—real sportsmen, I mean—are artistic; it is merely to apply that term logically, as it ought to be applied. A large part of the human race is covered in this way by an epithet usually vague and specialised, and so it ought to be. No difference in kind divides the individual who is commonly said to be artistic from the sportsman who is supposed not so to be. On the contrary, the sportsman is a recognisable kind of artist. So soon as pleasure is being pursued, not simply for its face value, as it is being pursued at this moment by the cook below, who is chatting with the fishmonger when I know she ought to be basting the joint, not in the simplest way, but for some more remote and emotional object, it partakes of the nature of Art. This distinction may easily be perceived in the world of sport. It points the difference between one who is content to paddle a boat by himself because he likes the exercise, or likes the sensation of occupying a boat upon the water, or wants to use the water to get to some desirable spot, and one who trains for a race; the difference between kicking a football and playing in a game of football; the difference between riding individually for the liver's sake and riding to hounds. Certainly neither the sportsman nor the mountaineer can be accused of taking his pleasure simply. Both are artists; and the fact that he has in view an emotional experience does not remove the mountaineer even from the devotee of Association football.

But there is Art and ART. We may distinguish amongst artists. Without an exact classification or order of merit we do so distinguish habitually. The 'Fine Arts' are called 'fine' presumably because we consider that all Arts are not fine. The epithet artistic is commonly limited to those who are seen to have the artistic sense developed in a peculiar degree.

It is precisely in making these distinctions that we may estimate what we set out to determine—the value of mountaineering in the whole order of our emotional experience. To what part of the artistic sense of man does mountaineering belong? To the part that causes him to be moved by music or painting, or to the part that makes him enjoy a game?

By putting the question in this form we perceive at once the gulf that divides the arrogant mountaineer from the sportsman. It seemed perfectly natural to compare a day in the Alps with a symphony. For mountaineers of my sort mountaineering is rightfully so comparable; but no sportsman could or would make the same claim for cricket or hunting, or whatever his particular sport might be. He recognises the existence of the sublime in great Art, and knows, even if he cannot feel, that its manner of stirring the heart is altogether different and vaster. But mountaineers do not admit this difference in the emotional plane of mountaineering and Art. They claim that something sublime is the essence of mountaineering. They can compare the call of the hills to the melody of wonderful music, and the comparison is not ridiculous.

* * *

Published as 'The Mountaineer as Artist'

Climber's Club Journal, March 1914.

2
MOUNTAIN CRAFT

It may be said at once that this is the most important work on mountaineering which has appeared in this generation. The statement is not strictly true, for it has not yet appeared.[1] But the long-deferred fulfilment of our hopes is at last within countable weeks. And we are not to be disappointed. The book is no less important than it sets out to be. It is all and more than all that we had a right to expect.

Mr G.W. Young, besides being the principal author, is also editor of a series of articles by collaborating hands. Experts have been pressed into the service. They supplement Mr Young in the matter of pure technique, Captain Farrar about equipment, A.H. Lunn about mountaineering on ski, and Sydney Spencer on photography; and they deal with regional peculiarities outside the Alps and the British Isles: Mr Wollaston with tropical countries, Mr Martin Conway with Spitzbergen, Mr Raeburn with the Caucasus, Mr George Finch with Corsica, Dr Longstaff with the Himalaya, Mr Slingsby with Norway, Mr Malcolm Ross with New Zealand, Mr Claud Elliott with the Pyrenees, and Mr Mumm with the Rocky Mountains. The editor presumably esteems it no small part of his success that he should have spurred his experts to such a high level of performance. He might indeed have added to his chapter on the art of managing an alpine party an appendix on the art of managing collaborators. Evidently they have been well managed, as they would no doubt admit—or even claim. The regional articles fulfil two functions. They are valuable introductions to the study of different regions where the mountaineer of leisure may project campaigns, or at least allow his arm-chair mind to summon imagined pleasures; and they summarize mountaineering experience in those regions for his practical guidance. I am myself of a practical turn of mind, and I shall keep this second part of *Mountain Craft*, so to speak, on the shelf, until I am actually making my plans for the Himalaya, or it may be Spitzbergen or Popocatapetl (which does not, however, appear in the index, where I hoped to make certain of its orthography). Nevertheless I have derived much enjoyment, and I hope some profit, from reading these chapters. It is a limited view of mountain craft that would look no farther than the British Isles and the Alps; the mountaineer who believes in his art will, presumably, pursue it for its own sake to these distant heights, even though he should prefer the word 'craft'.

I am not, as may be seen, attempting to review this work. Reviews are no less useful in the mountaineering than other worlds, as affording opportunities for the younger and humbler generation to make retort, with the customary jargon of Olympus, in qualified praise for advice received. It would be impossible, however, in this case to have the reviewer's satisfaction; for the weight of advice offered in these pages could be compensated by no amount of praise and qualification. And there is a further difficulty: I believe as little in impartial friendship as in partial criticism. I refuse to look down from Mount Olympus on Mr Young, because I have had the privilege of climbing mountains with him; and I should inevitably be condemned in the ascent by that standard of mountaineering tact which he lays down in this book.

I prefer to assume that the summit in question is occupied by him. He occupies it, I need hardly say, in the most graceful imaginable manner. It is not apparently a summit where he would wish to stay, and he seems unconscious of any such throne. The reader, however, can hardly forget the circumstance. Evidence is constantly accumulating before his eyes of remarkable qualities in Mr Young's ascent thither. The book is an ordered survey of mountaineering practice and principle; but it is no less a record of the author's experience, which lies behind all his theories and judgements, and is supremely interesting for that reason. To those who accept as a matter of course the brilliant record of an individual mountaineer and explain it to themselves by some simple formula—saying perhaps that it proceeds from a happy combination of gifts, an unrivalled enthusiasm, a splendid physique and a daring imagination—to casual critics, it may be surprising to learn by what detailed and patient art the results were achieved. The table of contents is itself a revelation. Eighty pages, we find, are devoted to 'Management and Leadership'; nearly fifty to 'Climbing in Combination'; more than twenty to 'Corrective Method', an analysis of the attitude and extraordinary precautions which prevent accidents; 'Reconnoitring' takes some thirty pages; and beyond all this the technique of snow and ice craft, of rock climbing and the use of guides, are subjects treated at length in separate chapters. And the method is nowhere diffuse; it is a concentrated, well-winnowed style packed with observation and illuminating analysis; a fullness based not only upon opportunities of experience, but upon experience itself that comes of mental alertness on every occasion and with regard to every detail of mountaineering practice; and upon reflection after the event stimulated by a conscious and insistent desire to discover principles where principles are discoverable, to master every aspect of a complicated art—one might almost say to create it.

In one direction, especially, Mr Young has indisputably created an art—in his psychological attitude towards mountaineering. He cares supremely for personal relations in a party of climbers. No previous writer has so emphasised their importance. Here chiefly, he persuades us, lies the secret of success, and he examines them courageously in detail, in the details even of what we call manners. The standard laid down is one with which we are familiar, that of civilised men not competing, but co-operating. It might seem at first sight hardly necessary to tell us, for instance, of the etiquette which should be observed as we walk a shepherd-track on a hill-side. But this point is fully dealt with. It is possible in some small ways to irritate a companion or on the other hand to promote comradeship. We must obviate the least occasion for friction and do everything for harmony. Smoking is enjoined for its social utility, so that a man may sustain his part in the 'effortless silence' which is a condition of comradeship, and chattering forbidden (how grateful I am for that!) whenever the leader is in stress of difficulties. Open rather than expressed criticism is advocated, and a law of reciprocity in abuse is hinted at, though scarcely formulated.

It is evident that the writer's emphasis on the minutiae of personal relations proceeds from a premise that the effort and concentration required by mountaineering inevitably string up nerves to a state of high tension. Everything must be done to guard against the dangers from mental stress. The first chapter on 'Leadership and Management' analyses the conditions under which these dangers may arise, the effects of boredom and ill-temper, the situations created by over-excitement and the causes of friction in a party, most dangerous when suppressed. It is possible by taking thought to avoid or at least to minimise the attendant evils; a climber by watching his own mental states, and those of his companions, may promote the collective confidence upon which the success and safety of all so largely depend. In the leader this duty is supremely important. And it should be his care, too, so to order the details of organisation as to rule out, so far as possible, the occasions of friction and worry.

Perhaps no prospect can be so appalling to the mountaineer as the volume and complexity of the matter about which he is required to think, especially if he be—neither manager nor leader quite hits the mark; I will say therefore—'boss' of a party. To read these pages at home in hours of well-merited repose after the strenuous and perhaps not simple mutations of an Alpine season, can lead to but one conclusion in any man who has taken a share, however humble, in controlling the climbing destinies of himself and his companions. His insufficiency is too manifest, it is probably notorious. He must abjure that leading role, absolutely and forever. Or he must pocket his pride and leave his hopes in the hotel, all the highest, all but the meanest. The ambition of great enterprises must be banished even from his dreams. For him there can remain, if he is to have any responsibility, only the association of stoical comrades who have determined by the same stern law with himself to travel where indeed one quality is demanded, the quality of patience, but none besides. Or, at best, he may be the humblest member of some sober party whose range of aspiration is one degree more adventurous. The rest is for men of leisure, or men of genius, or preferably for men of both, who have eleven months in the year for recreation after a month's ambitious and exhausting mountaineering, and an infinite capacity for becoming exhausted.

The inevitable pursuit of these gloomy reflections must lead at last to a ray of hope. The psychological art created by Mr Young (from the voice of an inward groan I seem to hear the suggestion), is it in reality created for us all or only perchance for Mr Young himself? Is it not possible that other men may achieve the same result by other methods—may learn by some broad gesture to sweep away complexity, to achieve a well-balanced and calm simplicity; and yet be competent, with the multifarious omnicompetence required of a modern leader bearing, in every and even the most trying situation, his companions' ill-temper and even his own? For my part I entertain no such illusion. I am convinced beyond argument by the writer's reasoning. For me the broad gesture could only mean the unshouldering of responsibilities in a golden dream. It may, and indeed it must be a personal question as to how exactly the approach shall be made, that delicate approach to comrades' spirits when they are excited in the heat of action, or cold from inactivity, or irritable from misadventure, or jaded from disappointment, or merely weary because the way is long and stones are tiresome or snow is deep. It is in the creed of every mountaineer that he should steel himself against the power of circumstances. But, as Mr Young tells us, he has a further duty: he must learn no less to steel others. There is no simple way of avoiding this care; it cannot be left to chance. Some climbers may be so fortunately compounded of sympathy, indifference, and invincible breeziness that their task will be comparatively light. But no one is so splendid on every occasion that he can afford to neglect the chance and the dangers of 'preventable humours'; and no simplification can secure for him without effort his own maximum coefficient of harmonious behaviour.

But if this thesis be not chimerical, and I think it is not, a small hope of escape may yet be found. Mr Young, though he advises fencing for the body as a 'training in rapid adjustments and lightning reactions', says nothing of any such training by fencing or otherwise for the mind. It is the one criticism of his book that I have to offer, and I offer it not in humility, but in pride. In the course of reading these chapters by the editor I found myself on more than one occasion discovering, as I thought, an omission, some further consideration that might have been added here or there; but invariably as I read on I found my own thought expressed elsewhere, given its proper dignity under a different heading, or introduced as a more apt illustration of a different point. It was an irritating experience seeing that I was projecting an article. But at last I have found an omission—the only one it surely must be; and since Mr Young has omitted to make any recommendation for the training of our minds I shall take upon myself the privilege of offering an unaided suggestion.

Alpine seasons are all too precarious and life too short for us to develop in the scenes where it is most required a sufficient measure of psychological adaptability. But something, I believe, might be done in England. A party, let us suppose, of four men might arrange to use the weekend opportunities for expeditions to be carried out under particular rules which would demand the exercise of the qualities to be induced. Imagine them on a Saturday or Sunday afternoon, on one of those days not infrequently provided by our temperate climate, with the temperature not so very low, but the air moist and raw; imagine them setting forth from the charming ease of a bright Surrey residence for the sufficiently distant ascent of Hindhead, and envisaging at the end the cosy reward of comfortable afternoon tea. Two of them will be clothed as it were for midsummer, in the gauziest garments short of indecency, and two as it were for the Arctic, muffled in furs; two will be equipped as to the feet with sand shoes, and two with Carter's Dreadnoughts; one of each pair will carry a portentous rucksack; and the leader will have been chosen by mutual consent as being the man who is freest from prejudice about the route, and by the same token knows least about it. All are pledged to abide by these conditions, and it has been further arranged that they shall be overtaken on the way by a succession of sumptuous motor-cars, whose great-hearted occupants will offer them the bounty of a lift. The climax arrives when they find these motorists, whose offers they necessarily disdained according to their own hard rules, in occupation of every haven convenient for their repose. I suggest that these not impossible conditions, with their by no means improbable end, and not least the imaginable situations *en route*, would afford opportunities for preliminary training in reciprocal mentality. Mountaineers, I trust, not less earnest, and more ingenious than myself, will contrive a system by some such devices—a system whose aim is no more than a habit, but a habit whose service is the higher harmony.

Mr Young will forgive me, I hope, if I labour this theme too much. It has coloured his writing so distinctly—I don't say so highly—it is so arresting, so important, and has consequences so far-reaching in our whole attitude towards mountaineering, that one neither treats it lightly nor lightly abandons it. Nowhere perhaps is it so important as in all he tells us about guides in the Alps, their training, their mental attitude, and their worth; and in no part of this book is he more profoundly wise and more convincing than where he speaks from experience and study uniquely interesting of the relations that may and should and do exist between guides and amateurs. He neither condemns nor recommends guideless climbing. All depends on the party and the expedition in view. His interest is to determine with regard to these conditions, firstly, under what circumstances a guide should be taken, and, secondly, in what way responsibility should be divided between professional leader and amateur director. No such detailed discussion, so far as I know, of the guide and his uses has been published before, and no man who takes mountaineering seriously can afford to neglect it. The study of this book may lead him to alter his practice in more respects than one, and not least in this matter of guides.

On more purely technical questions Mr Young is more authoritative, and yet hardly less personal. The experience of climbers in the pure craft of climbing has been crystallised to a point where authority is undisputed about many matters of importance. The accomplished mountaineer, while he is grateful for the clear statement of much that has never before been stated, will find himself agreeing very largely with the author. But he will scarcely be less interested for that reason; and he may usefully ask himself such a question as—How many climbers of my acquaintance still sit, whenever they can find a seat, to bring up the man below, or how many are really competent to make proper use, in the manner so carefully explained, of unsound holds? The chapter on 'Ice Craft' especially will meet with general agreement; as to the use of crampons, the manner of walking in steps, the correct way of cutting them, besides much else. But beyond an almost undebatable ground, individual judgment has a large part to play. Opinions differ, for instance, as to the correct use of the rope on ice. Mr Young lays it down quite definitely as a general rule that the pick should not be used as a belay in hard ice, and maintains that the rope should be held in the hand; he rejects the theory that a slip cannot be checked on ice except by using the axe, and contemplates the possibility, or perhaps even the probability, that it may be checked by a climber who remains firmly balanced in his step and can ease the jerk with his arm. As experience on this head is not generally sought, it would be interesting to know what have been Mr Young's experiences, and those of any climber who has succeeded in checking a slip on ice. It is only by detailed consideration of such points that we can arrive at safe method in climbing.

The most audacious section of this chapter deals with glacier work. It corresponds, no doubt, to audacity in practice. If the reader has felt elsewhere perhaps a trifle chilled by the restraints imposed upon him, he is warmed by encouragement when he will be most in need of it. With favouring circumstances he is urged forward into the intricacies of a broken glacier, among 'the wettest, bluest, and nastiest-looking *séracs*.... With a good axe, good claws, and a good friend, to set one's foot on the crisp spring of moving ice and feel battle joined with the white, blue, and silver giants of a glacier fall, I know no excitement so sanely joyous; and no sound so thrilling as the clean, hollow smack of axe and the bell-like rustle of the falling ice-chips returning from the deep crevasse; and yet again, no exultation more healthy than to look back through the glittering labyrinth of turquoise and grey precipice, of sapphire chasm, fretted spire, and lucent arch, flake and buttress, and see the little serpent of our blurred blue steps edged with the tiny winking prisms of sunlit ice-dust, soaring, dipping, circling, hazarding on its absurd adventure; surely a connected thread of very happy human purpose, asserting its gay consequence triumphantly through the heart of the wildest and most beautiful of the conflicts between nature's silent armies.' The happy human purpose, of course, might have an unhappy end. But why should it? We can see and appreciate the dangers; there are none uncountable here; we can avoid the malice of those we know.

The essence of Mr Young's teaching about safety lies here. We must distinguish between the knowable and the unknowable dangers; these knowable ones we must probe and calculate to the farthest point, we must become fully conscious of them all, and take our precautions accordingly. For the unknown and unknowable we must have, as we say, our margin. Nothing is more difficult to contrive in practice on big mountains. But there is a way even to this; it is the way of speed. A section of this book is devoted to 'Pace', and it is perhaps the most valuable of all; the power and practice of pace by sustained rhythm (and not by a headlong rush) is the biggest factor of efficiency in a party, and there can have been no greater service to mountaineering than Mr Young's advocacy of this thesis. Probably many of us at different times have felt vague doubts about it. If we develop speed shall we not sacrifice safety—some factor of restraint which is in itself a precaution? And shall we not lower the whole value of our pursuit by sacrificing enjoyment itself—some quality of contemplation which is so much the essence of enjoyment that the mere suggestion of hurting it alarms us, and we hold up our hands with horror at the picture presenting itself in antithesis, the American tourist in his automobile. But Mr Young answers these questions with complete success. By pace he means a synthetic movement actuated by a finer concentration and advancing rhythmically, with a rhythm more definitely imposed and more compelling, so that we attain in our progress a more perfect touch, a more absorbing harmony with all that is about us; as our contacts are made more swiftly, perception too is quickened, and the contacts themselves are more accurate; they are more accurate so long as we retain rhythm, for rhythm is the necessary control and fixes the limit of acceleration for the individual climber. Thus we may proceed not with more danger, but with less, not with less enjoyment, but with more, so far as climbing is concerned, while we save time for what is enjoyed incidentally, for the unhurried halt in the later stages, the pipe of unshadowed peace when the end is assured; and we secure our safety; we can spend our saved time on the great difficulties, or we have it to spend for the unforeseen.

I cannot turn from this chapter without one regret. I could wish the author had allowed himself to express—though it was beside his technical point—something of his personal response, to twinkle with his gay crystal phrases, ring the silver bells for us, and make us leap a little in the delight of mere motion with his poetry of speed—the swiftness which is indeed untamed when we march with the west wind, but not uncontrollable, and prouder on a mountain side, a 'skiey speed', but not insensible. He has, alas(!) inhibited what must have been his impulse.

But he has not spared his hand when he comes to 'Reconnaissance', and I find no part of his book more agreeable. I have always said to myself that I have a good eye for a mountain, and explained the matter quite simply. I look at mountains geometrically. It sounds a lamentably unpoetical statement and has required some courage: but one sometimes discovers agreement in unexpected quarters. Mr Young has revealed himself also as a geometrician, or perhaps I should rather say 'cubist', with regard to mountains. He sees them as a complicated problem in lines and angles, a sort of stupendous 'rider'. It is true that I find here little enough support for my premise. My eye perhaps is less good than I thought it. I am for the most part satisfied to observe intuitively. But Mr Young is conscious of his interferences; he classifies them and tells us how they are made. He tells me how many of mine own are made, and not only delights me by the process, but encourages me to think I may observe more in the future. His own observations at all events are no less numerous than interesting, and the reason is that he is so keenly conscious of the process—and also of course that he sees the mountain as a 'rider'. Would that I could expound this art of his at greater length—but that must be left for a future article entitled, 'The Cubist Movement in Orosophy Unmasked'.

Of the other articles, that by Mr Spencer on photography is probably in its sphere no less authoritative. Of that I am quite unable to judge, though I believe I can appreciate to the full his glorious frontispiece. It may be said, however, that the least expert of amateur photographers may learn a great deal from Mr Spencer, and the experienced photographer will find much to interest him.

Captain Farrar on equipment is another authority not to be questioned where mountaineering practice has established anything; and his article is full of useful information as to what is the best of its kind and how to obtain it. On the delicate question of boots' comfort, however, there are limits within which it is impossible to lay down indisputable laws. We may all agree that they should fit round the instep, be roomy in the toes, and have narrow welts; but feet are individual, and when it comes to a test for the toes that they should have room to 'crumple up inside the boot' one suspects that opinions may differ. For my part I can't say offhand whether or not my toes would crumple up; but I suspect they wouldn't, and that I should be sorry if they could. And I can say that I have tried socks, socks of cork, of leather, and of fibre, on a number of occasions; but far from endorsing the practice Captain Farrar recommends, I have come to a determination to eschew them utterly. As to nails no two climbers may be expected to agree, and I am certain no one will agree with me. Tricounis, for all that may be said in their favour, do wear down—to an abominable smooth hard surface, which may indeed give the best grip on pudding, but not on anything worthy to be called rock. And yet they have quite special advantages. Accordingly I prefer a hotchpotch—a selection of the most beautiful nails artistically arranged to meet all sorts of contingencies. And raiment, lastly, how impossible to standardise! For raiment again is individual, as Mr

Young is the first to admit, for he inserts by Captain Farrar's permission certain 'alternative suggestions' which are an invaluable record of his personal habits. I confess I agree with both and yet with neither of these experienced mountaineers, and I hope the time may never come when I must entirely agree with either. For then I should be compelled on the one hand to wear a waistcoat, a garment I could only bring myself to wear when 'frozen frore' in hell-fire's icy alternative, or, on the other hand, discard my warmest friend, the blessed shirt and in either case I should have to abandon my plus fours, the latest incontrovertible delight, and abandon too, I fear, as the final reserve in my rucksack, a shirt of fine-spun silk.

One more chapter remains to be mentioned, Mr Lunn's about mountaineering on ski. It is admirable for compressing a large matter into a small space and an illuminating introduction to a most interesting subject. As I have never visited the Alps in winter and don't propose to ski there in summer, I will say no more. The regional articles, it is to be hoped, will find their measure of appreciation and criticism in a future number of this journal, or in that larger and more splendid organ to be created by the united will of mountaineering clubs.

Meanwhile Mr Young still sits on Mount Olympus and is equally tired of sitting and of the view. He will descend of course by the method he describes, and his readers too, who have followed him in these high places, will climb down regretfully, but still delighted, through the pages of his collaborators by the 'pleasure of quick light contacts', among mountains from Spitzbergen to New Zealand, down 'like the spokes of a revolving rimless wheel', gaily and happily, wiser but not too wise, nor in any sense fatigued, ready when they meet his smile on the plains again to be kindled once more to a fresh desire for mountains, sane mountains, sane enterprise, and sane companions. * * *

Review of Geoffrey Winthrop Young's *Mountain Craft*

Climber's Club Journal, December 1920.

3

NONE BUT OURSELVES
Mont Maudit, 1916

The expedition recorded in the following pages came as the culminating event for three fit men in the splendid August of 1911. The
party were R.L.G. Irving, H.B.G. Tyndale, and G. Mallory, the present writer. They believed themselves to be making the second
ascent of Mont Blanc from the Col de la Tour Bonde over Mont
Maudit. In point of fact it was probably the third.

We knew only of Burgener's party of 1887. They—Herr v.
Kuffner, Alexander Burgener, and two other men—had started
from a bivouac on the Mont de la Brenva and followed the narrow
arête crossed by the Col de la Tour Ronde, near which they
bivouacked a second night.[2] Their account was very present in our
minds both in planning the expedition and in achieving the ascent.

The second ascent,[3] we subsequently learned, was made by SS
Canzio and Nondini with Henri Brocherel in August 1901.

It is not often, I suppose, that a member of the Alpine Club
finds himself, several years after the event, writing the account of
an expedition in the Alps from an unaided memory. Perhaps it is
overbold to attempt such a thing. But, since I am determined to
attempt it, I have ventured to adopt for literary aid an unusual

form—one that differs from the straightforward narrative commonly used in this Journal to express the facts of adventure; a form better fitted as I think to express rather distant memories among which few details survive and are clearly seen; happily a few such do still exist—but many thoughts and feelings. I have chosen it for another reason too. In the May number of this year's (1917) *Alpine Journal* I read an article by my friend R.L.G. Irving, in which he told us about the first battle in the Alps of two young men, since killed at the front. And, 'Happy men,' I thought, 'that they met the Alps first.' Perhaps I was not alone in making that mental exclamation. At least I cannot doubt that many would approve the thought—many of the younger members who have shared the common lot of young men at present, who have lived in grim and desolate scenes and been comforted by mountains. For it may happen that mountains too distant to be seen present themselves beautifully to the imagination for wholesome cheer; and it has seemed to me that an expedition, the memory of which has been a friendly companion, ought properly to be connected with those unbeautiful places where I have best remembered it.

Pages from a Journal
France, Autumn 1916

Dreariness, Monotony, Sloth! These I suppose should be the headings of the new chapter. Truly the rains have come and the season of opaque mists; the spells of long, damp waiting and cold inaction. An adjustment is necessary. Perhaps G.H.Q. will oblige with a pamphlet, 'Rules for the sober fortitude of those who prefer excitement'. How do men exist, I wonder, the zest of action almost extinguished? 'Boredom', that odious and too common word! Do they go back simply to that? Thank God, I'm not bored. Perhaps men only pretend to be bored because they think it unmanly to be childishly amused; secretly perhaps they indulge visions of delight. In any case I'll be nothing but grateful for my visions, grateful for the supreme good fortune of Alpine memories. I can look long at my mountains without being bored. And yet it is not wholly satisfying merely to look at them. However sharply I distinguish those mountain-scenes a certain vagueness remains to be dispersed. And why not clear it up—see one vision clearly in its true perspective of deeper suggestion? I will record for my own intenser light, one splendid day, all the facts and thoughts, as I remember them now, completely and exactly. Facts and thoughts! A mere jumble at first sight as I look back. Do the facts exist for me independently? If I view them detachedly, as historically happening to historical people, the Graham, the Harry and the me of five years ago, they seem to lose their significance, to have no interest for me, no meaning. I can bring myself with an effort to think about them like that, but it is not so that I remember them. They passed into my mind, not as things that I witnessed, but as thoughts that came to me. What more after all are the events of life than moments in the stream of thought, which is experience? It is the experience, in this sense, of an Alpine expedition that I want to recall. But can I recall it? As the day even now begins to take more definite shape before me, I find not only reasoned thoughts such as may easily be expressed in words, but thought less tangible, less precise, thought that would rather be called feeling. A stream of feeling I seem to recall. But am I feeling now what I felt then? I can't be sure of that. Perhaps, through the strange contrast between those scenes and this world about me, my present emotion is further from the cold light of reason; I am troubled by the marvellous reappearance of so much lost beauty, so many loved shapes. And then, being human, I am subject to change; each day the sum of experience adds up to a different total. Decidedly the total of today is not that of five years ago; probably an emotion can never be exactly repeated or reproduced; the same chords may be struck, the music has altered tones. And yet there is ultimate truth in experience recalled—if not quite recaptured. It is only from what was originally thought and felt that any present emotion exists. The past may live again—with a difference; and what lives is true. And if I am condemned, in spite of all my remembrance, to see that day through the more travelled eyes of now, it can only live for me again through those other eyes—the eyes of one who stood in the sun and looked upwards with fear and hope, and who sat in the shade of rocks with half a world beneath his feet; I must stand where *he* stood in the sun, sit where *he* sat in the shade; inhabit the places where he most intently thought and felt and there look through his eyes.

Up and beyond a great tower of rock, not long after midday, he surveyed the first stage of the expedition duly accomplished. The efforts of climbing had been exhausting; now his limbs were folded restfully against the rocks where he lay niched beneath a granite wall; their dragging weight no longer counted. An unconsciousness almost of sleep had all his tired body and his spirit had the freedom of dreams.

The hewn forms on every side defined themselves insistently; there was pain in seeing them so acutely, like seeing suddenly into a man's soul, full of strange beauty and sorrow. The walls of a vast couloir guarding this side of the Brenva; the Brenva glacier itself, and beyond; the Péteret—all this world of white and black and blue loomed more and more fantastic. He seemed to hear the hiss of a monster steam-saw cutting the titanic members for a world of ice and rocks. Then came utter riot and chaos. He opened his eyes again and saw things normally. A spirit of insolence took him. Those straight-cut rocks beyond the basin of snow, how smooth and steep! Probably vertical! They meant to be terrible. Yet men existed, he would wager, able to conquer them, who would, perhaps, scale them…. And the Brenva (he noted the exact curve with which the ice arête bit the slope)…. What was it? A staircase for men to walk up and down. Lies, all lies! To think at all of mountains in such terms was a lie. The whole mood was a lie, mean, vaunting, blasphemous…. The dignity and peace of mountains from height to depth, from sunlight to shadow! The still glory of such a host, unmasked and beautiful? All the patience and wisdom of the ages seemed to be graven here, all the courage and endurance and all the travail. These forms had listened to the jar of terrible discords and the music of gentle voices, had seen the hard strokes of cruelty and the forgiving gesture of pity. They could be greatly troubled yet splendidly serene, they could threaten, but also smile. These faces hid the depths of doubt and faith, of hate and love. They knew the energy of doing and the calm of repose; the stormy tossing of endeavour and the even keel of achievement; they knew the shades of care and the frank way of kindly laughter; anxiety and the quiet reaches of thought; slow pain and swift delight. They knew, changing with snow and wind and sun, the flicker of quick response to a thousand moods, and, with all this complex heart, had the strength of great resolves unchanging; a constant spirit immutably clean and true and friendly. Here tortured pride, perhaps, would find the infinite wrath and infinite despair; but here, too, among the mountains would be found infinite hope and steps for children's feet…. Unchanging, and so still! Had the great heart stopped beating? Were the eternal whisperings silent? He saw three figures on a mountain's limb, flies on the carved thigh of a giant, waiting. Would they move again? It seemed more fitting that they should stay there always, himself in his rocky niche and the others perched just so. He became aware of a companion close at hand—Graham, preparing some soup. There was a purpose here; they would be going forward again presently and up. Was it this man's will? His own seemed to have no part in the matter—or was it a kind of destiny, something which they all obeyed necessarily?

Go on? Yes, perhaps; granted for the moment the possibility of that. But by what sort of miracle had he got so far? He went back to the ideas of yesterday. From more than one point of view Graham and he had gazed upon this limb of Mont Maudit, on the very place where they now were most intently; for wasn't it the knot of the whole expedition? They had prophesied no great difficulties below the tower, and that could surely be circumvented one way or another; the most formidable obstacle, as it appeared from below, was the steep rock wall above; but it ought to go—this wonderful granite was always split somewhere; they would find a way. So they had talked; but for him, and for Graham too no doubt, the features of this expedition had taken tremendous shapes in the unspoken mind. Had he not gone to bed with toes and fingers tingling, tremulous, expectant, half-afraid, yet filled with the thought of a great hope to be realised? And how dismay had followed his first sensations of the early morning! The cause of the trouble lay in that innocent-looking meal overnight—pleasant meal, eaten in high spirits and with little jests that sparkled in the mirror of mountain friendships. Sour wine or dirty water? It had been a difficult choice after a dry day. He didn't blame himself for choosing wine, and decidedly not for immoderate potations of that discouraging beverage. Nevertheless, disaster came of the sour wine, new wine it was said to be. Damn new wine! What a shadow had fallen on big dreams when he woke in the morning and knew that big stomach was upset. He had made a start as a matter of course, not that he thought it anywise possible to go far that day, but it was necessary to demonstrate the impossibility. They had started punctually in the first light, about four o'clock. He was very glad of that; he wouldn't easily forgive himself for delaying a start. But in the very first steps over the almost level snow of the Col du Géant how heavily his legs had dragged, and what a weak, incompetent performance since. And yet what an ideal start! No track-hunting by lantern light, not a step of troublesome moraine, not even a dry glacier—not that such things hadn't their places too, but they belonged to a less elevated order. Today a splendid field of snow had led them from the outset to this great world of wonders; only one other start in his memory, for the grandeur of the scene and for pure physical joy, ought to be compared to that, when two of the same party had started for the Dent Blanche from the Col de Bertol. But that glorious snow-field was an Alpine highway. Today, from the moment when they had turned over the lip and down into the deep basin below the Col de la Tour Ronde, had been distinguished by their seeming to have severed themselves even from the haunts of climbers. He had noticed these sensations rather than enjoyed them. Not much physical delight had come to him. As they mounted towards the col it had seemed impossible even to climb so far. While still on the gentle snow, before they had begun seriously to ascend, it had come to him bitterly how different from the living dreams of yesterday was the dead reality. Hopes! There was no room for hope. It was degrading to be the slave of mere physical conditions; be hated as a personal enemy the domination of the material. And yet he had succeeded in thinking only of how to struggle on and how not to be sick.

So it had been with almost unbroken continuity up to the time of their first halt. The choice of route had come up among them and afforded a passing interest. Their ideas had seemed rather hazy as to where exactly was the Col de la Tour Ronde; but what did it matter? The arête leading to their desired buttress seemed accessible at many points on that side, and the obvious line was the nearest to their objective; there had been no great difficulty in reaching a shallow couloir, and once attained this simple channel had brought them out on the buttress well above the arête. A short discussion about falling stones had condemned the couloir for the purpose of retreat; even that small flutter of interest had served to break the spell and been strangely exhilarating—as though there were really a question of playing today that old game with the mountains. But the time had been long—nearly three hours from the start for what seemed no great achievement, and when they disposed themselves at last for breakfast he had still no thoughts beyond his heart-breaking sensations—of lifting bars of lead and tugging bags of ore a long way up over snow and rocks.

Breakfast had been a lengthy meal—or rather it had provided a long halt, an hour and a quarter instead of the usual forty minutes—prolonged by a misadventure, if misadventure it was; a stone inadvertently dislodged had upset the seething mess of porridge. Graham, notorious the Alps over for an irrepressible passion for brewing things, had been distinctly annoyed though not very expressively—as indeed he had every right to be, since he, evidently, was to bear the brunt of whatever might turn up—and had at once re-established the pot with additions of snow and oats. Harry, however, had shown much sympathy for the author of the delay; perhaps he had experienced a spasm of not quite regretting it; and his attitude had contrived to establish or at all events to foreshadow an alliance of weakness; not that Harry had any need for such, but he had a way of staking out a claim in advance, a sort of insurance against the frailty of human nature; so here would be an ear open in the last resort. It was a comfortable feeling.

But there was more comfort than that. There was rest, not the least of the rewards. And there was beauty. He didn't precisely feel that these places were more beautiful than others. What use in comparing absolutes except to appreciate quality? This was conspicuously unlike many of the most beautiful mountain scenes, which are often dominated by the sheer lyrical force or the rugged magnificence of a single peak—so that one *must* look at the Weisshorn, it may be, or the Matterhorn, or the Dent Blanche. Here an enchanted host surrounded him. Probably every one who knew them had a place apart, as he had, in the imagination for the great members of Mont Blanc; their spell captured and held his mind during the first halt; not only the impression of what he immediately saw, beautiful as it was, but the sense of all that was suggested and could be said actually to be present because there seemed to be no limits. Therefore, so long as he had stayed just looking and wondering, feeling breadth and height and space, the personal question had been put aside. The end was still unthinkable; he had banished all agitating speculation on that head, not caring to be perplexed. To be there! Nothing else mattered. And though no hope of the expedition had been born then, he had received an assurance of the day. The great thing had happened; the spirit had its flight; and the rest must take care of itself.

The problems of action, however, had their whole alarming value when the party moved on again. Breakfast, so far as he was concerned, had not been a success. He cast no aspersions upon the victuals; but with him they had been unfortunate. He had acquired no strength for what lay ahead. Graham went in front as before, and himself next on the rope. Rocks and snow were in good condition, and they were helped by the fierce little points of their crampons. For a long distance no big cause of delay kept them back. For him it had been chiefly a matter of keeping up—easier on rocks where his arms could help. Occasionally a more difficult passage had allowed him to wait while the leader went on alone and while Harry came up after him. But neither of them wasted time. He had moments of wishing that these men of steel could show some signs of fatigue, but their attitude discouraged weariness. It had been a relief to come upon a narrow arête; the angle was less steep and it was not a place to hurry.

Then they had been confronted by the great tower. It was a climax; a blessed climax! The old mountain was showing fight. Graham had invited his counsel; he had taken heart of that grace; to be consulted fitted in with his formulae for himself. He had a passion for projecting possible routes and always held a view about the best line. It had been evident almost at first sight that they could turn this obstacle on the left. Graham had pointed out that way. But it would take time to cut steps round there and they would still have to regain the crest beyond, which might prove difficult. To Graham's deliberations he had therefore suggested an alternative plan. From their position they might climb on to a conspicuous shoulder on the right side of the gendarme; and from there they would be able to judge whether it was possible to make a way along that side, or even, conceivably, to climb over the top. Half an hour might be wasted, but they stood to save much more than that if an easy alternative was found. This suggestion had been adopted; but the half-hour had slipped away with no good result. They had then proceeded to turn the tower on its left side—a matter quite happily accomplished, though not without a struggle up a steep little chimney before they had gained access to their present halting-place. It was while Graham was cutting steps for the traverse that an unheard-of and almost unthinkable thing had happened. The second man, planted on a ledge, and hugging the rock round which he was belaying the rope, had fallen asleep. He had been woken by the sound of Harry's voice (Harry was round a corner) warning him to pay out the leader's rope. How long had he slept? Perhaps only for a few seconds—not longer in any case than since the rope was last paid out. Harry had been amused and sympathetic, and Graham had made light of the incident. But that didn't alter the fact. He had slept at his post—a responsible post too. So far as concerned the rope, he was inclined to think that, if a pull *had* come, he would have worked the belay instinctively: but if he had fallen....

He was going over all this in his mind as he lay in his niche facing the great tower. It had been a tale of incompetence all along. He had just let slip the handle of the boiler which was now, presumably, lying at the bottom of the black shaft between his feet—if there was a bottom to it. He was particularly annoyed by this act of folly. 'No care,' he was saying to himself, 'no care.' But in this mood another question had to be decided. That lapsed half-hour! It was clear enough as he saw it that the right side of the gendarme (left side as he looked back at it now) was impassable—a sheer, slippery precipice. Had that suggestion of his been as foolish as it looked? Had his judgment as a mountaineer been at fault? It had not been an occasion to throw away half an hour lightly. He confessed that it had been a chimerical sort of hope that entertained at all the idea of climbing over the top; it was in too icy a state just where one wanted it clean. And mightn't he have inferred those steep walls from the structure of the crest? He became convinced that in his suggestion had lurked a personal motive. The sequel proved it. Why had exhaustion overcome him exactly there and then? True, it had seemed to him a very strenuous half-hour: but it wasn't only that; it wasn't merely a physical fact that he had succumbed to sleep; it must be interpreted as the collapse of 'morale'. And it came just then— quite naturally as a reaction. He had wanted a supreme exhilaration; it was for that he had harboured the hope of a steeper way, more sensational. Such a way might possibly have been found; and the stimulus of such to the imagination and to the nerves would, he felt sure, have kept him going.

But what was to keep him going now—since evidently he was fated to go on? The course of these reflections brought him sharply back to face that problem, the immediate problem which must be resolved. He couldn't any longer proceed like an automaton; that way had been tried and failed. A change of mind, or rather a change of heart, was wanted. The day, if it were to be saved, must save him; he must feel its full Alpine significance. Somehow he must be strung up afresh to the task; emphatically some stimulus was required. But stimulus he felt was not to be had for the asking; one must proceed delicately to net that bird and feign indifference to his approach. His mood was still dominated by that strange incident on the traverse and the sense of his guilt. At all events nothing of that sort must occur again. He must establish a different state of being for Graham and Harry if not for himself. His companions—what was their attitude in these circumstances? How were they looking at the whole expedition? How did they stand as a party?

It was a critical situation seen whole—not that they had yet met with anything like a reverse; the conditions had been singularly favourable—perfect weather; rocks and snow as one would wish to find them. It was proving an easier course than might have been expected. One formidable difficulty mentioned in the scanty records of the previous party had been dealt with very happily. All had gone well so far, undoubtedly. But how far? So much lay in that question. They had all along to reckon with the salient facts that the one party before them had been obliged to sleep on the mountain. It was chiefly a matter of time. They had made about half the height from the Col de la Tour Ronde to the place where they expected to reach the true arête of Mont Maudit. Put down four hours for that; it hadn't taken less. How long would the next stage take? The steepest section lay immediately ahead of them, and therefore presumably the pace for a time would be slower. Put that against the big tower, which had taken time, and cancel the rest; it would be foolish to count less than four hours to the arête. They were not expecting difficulties once the arête was gained to the top of Mont Maudit; that part might take an hour or it might take two. Allow an hour and a half for it—five hours and a half so far. By this calculation they ought to find themselves on the summit of Mont Maudit about six o'clock. So far as safety went that was not one of the most alarming prospects; they could presumably get down by the corridor without much difficulty even in this year of open glaciers and join, so to speak, the high road to Chamonix; with the sort of tracks they expected to find after those weeks of fine weather they could make the Grand Mulets almost in the dark. True, the two and a half hours that might be called daylight, from 6 to 8.30 p.m., were not a very large margin for that performance. He broached the subject of time to his companions—but they put it off, for the best of reasons; there could be no question yet of retreat; they had still two hours at least before they must go on or sleep out. They could postpone considering time till the crisis arrived. (Perhaps, he thought, they would postpone it even then.) They were going forward now, and for the present his calculation was beside the point. Blessed Mont Blanc was their object and not Maudit Mont.

This simple reflection, now that he felt its force, seemed to work a miracle. Suddenly the required stimulus came and the change of heart; the spell of a great Alpine adventure took and held him. At last his fluttering thoughts had spread their wings and flown strongly to the summit. Here the three of them were sitting in the knot of all their difficulties; there lay the goal, a queen among mountains; there the white dome-like top so remotely poised. The clear features of that wonderland came to his eyes again; the tumbling waves of ice and blue precipices, winding glaciers wide and narrow, large rolling seas of snow; mysterious shy peaks and overbold ones, firm limbs of glowing rock, great sawing crests 'gap-toothed'. He now regarded these amazing phenomena with a sort of spiritual greed. Perhaps since food still had done nothing for him he was looking to the mountains simply for strength. These hewn creatures of ice and rock could inspire the most 'dull of soul'; he began somehow to feel strong. He had very different feelings now from those of half an hour ago. Yet these emotions could hardly be understood except as added to those; for those had been rather like worship without praise and these perhaps were the complement. He had felt the universe before rather as one within its clutch than as one living in it; if a pulse in the eternal mind, then a pulse that didn't beat. His mood had changed now. A place for the feet of children? Yes: but the children must bestir themselves; they may still be children. His perception of the universe had led him to heroics; he had travelled that old, old road; for isn't the passionate pilgrim a hero? He was re-established now in purpose and confidence; he had ceased to be the mere mainspring of a grumbling machine, of legs and arms that seemed hardly to belong to him; he was a man again, one of a party. It was no longer a case of being the least of a fool one could; he was prepared to play a part and there was a part to be played. His praise was that of one who functions sweetly and well—at least in spirit.

The battle in fact was more than half won from the moment this purpose and hope inspired him. It may be harder to think oneself to the top of a mountain than to pull oneself so far. Their knot still remained to cut, and physical problems had to be resolved. But his imagination overrode the details; he argued serenely that if he had won so high he could win the rest—poor reasoning perhaps, but largely true and justified in the result. The rocks helped magnificently. Like the shell of a walnut pinched with exactly the correct strength, the surface of the mountain cracked delicately but firmly, presented convenient fissures. The tired man could have met nothing more suitable. So many muscles could be charged with the task. A method of heaving against the legs, like an oarsman, often helped him up surprisingly. In all it was exhilarating work. He had a sense of splendid combination; the rope was never in the way; the party was moving rhythmically; there was delight in the long reaching up and swift, eager advance. It was sufficiently swift; they had slightly overrated the distance perhaps, but they found themselves within hail of the crest in no more than an hour and a quarter, and in half an hour more they were on it. The crest, however, was not gained without surmounting a difficult pitch—there was a climax, a pause, and, for him, a fresh crop of deliberations. He was standing in one of the final steps, hewn in the ice by Graham with infinite 'verve', which led up to a steep rock wall some twenty feet high. The wall presented itself in continuation of their stairway, so there was no gauging the obstacle till it was fairly reached. Would it go? And if not? The summit of Mont Blanc was a long way off; they still wanted all their time. An alternative might, and surely would, be found if necessary; but no other way had commended itself as simple and none was likely to be so short as this one. The issue would be decided by saving precious moments: there was every chance of wasting them in plenty. And was the party absolutely safe? The waiting strain emphasised his own exhaustion. His physical faith was staunch. But he experienced the conjectures that almost simulate doubt though the mind's trust too may be steadfast. He had no particle of doubt now; he stood absolutely for Graham with a crowd of recollections. Still, it was an uncomfortable place. The rocks, which came down just to his level, offered no belay, and not much holding for the one hand able to grasp them; and the ice-axe was no help. Not much chance, even for a strong man, of fielding the leader. And no better position offered unless a large platform were to be hewn up there from which to poke the first man into safety. It was nothing so very alarming or sensational after all—a tense moment, no more. But he came to see then, with peculiar clearness, what a fine ethic it was that bade him make a duty of these sombre conjectures and duly weigh them; put them alongside his trust for the leader and pass judgement. For the second man, besides ensuring the leader's safety in life and limb with every conceivable precaution, has also the party to defend, for the safety of all, against the leader's possible errors. Besides staking his uttermost farthing on that man he has positively to keep his conscience.

They paused on the arête—it can't be said that they halted—paused for a slackening of muscles and to gauge the situation. They looked up at the snow-slope rising in front of them to the summit of Mont Maudit, and saw that it was good—hard snow and not too steep; their crampons would easily deal with that surface. At three o'clock they were moving up again. For him the physical problem now presented a new form, and more disquieting. The difficulty had seemed chiefly to be in the weakness of his legs; he had been saved from utter disgrace before by the accommodating way of the mountain which had enabled him to use four limbs for hoisting. But now he could use only two. More than ever it had become a question of keeping up. Happily he remained supremely undepressed. A confidence that the day was won already dawned; the horizon had cleared. Moreover he derived comfort from observing his companions; they were beginning to lose that masterly air of being physically equal to everything. To his sharpened eye for such qualities it was remarkable that Graham lingered now and then in his step; and

Harry had reached the stage of emitting significant sounds. Since his own trouble rapidly came to a point when the legs unaided refused categorically to make the required push, these signs [they were not omens] from his companions encouraged his pride and strengthened his faith that a way would be found. A way *was* found. The arms again came to the rescue. He drove in the axe's pick at a convenient height; and, with the inner hand pressing on the shaft, was able to pull himself up; the device succeeded beyond hope; it seemed as though an invisible machine were helping him; with each step at the moment of transferring the balance his hands were somehow caught—and he was drawn quietly upwards. The monotonous machine seemed tired but worked sufficiently. Monotony was in the essence of this method; only he felt by a slow, repeated rhythm could he reach the summit.

They lay at last on the broad welcome spaces of the Col de la Brenva. It was a place of safety and enjoyment, wide and comfortable. Such noble amplitude was due from Mont Blanc. The divine sculptor, as Gibbon might have observed, after laboriously carving a multitude of gigantic shapes seemed in a moment of serene satisfaction to have designed a high imperial couch of purest snow. Here they must lie in delicious ease to stretch hard-worked muscles, to enjoy the high value of well-earned repose, and to drain the sunny cup of pleasure in contented peace. Much lay behind and beneath them. They had reached a brink of things—of all that lay, beyond sight, on the Brenva side falling into that steep Italian valley, and of the long slopes of snow and glacier stretching into France and into the lovely vale of Chamonix. Northwards lay all the spiky bed of aiguilles; to the S. the smooth white dome. How near they were to fulfilling all their hopes! They had but to put out their hands and take the crown offered. This pause, it might seem, had been given to them to taste beforehand the final triumph in full confidence of anticipation; and to rejoice without restraint in the full measure of achievement. Any party that reaches the Col de la

Brenva from Mont Maudit or still more from the Brenva Glacier must halt here with peculiar satisfaction. Perhaps, because thoughts of achievement would be scarce decent on the summit, one is presented with the opportunity of thinking them here. For his own part it was by no means wasted. However, in the course of pleasurable anticipation the white lump at some moments seemed alarmingly big. His companions did not pretend that it was small. But there remained with the party a certain sparkle of energy, a brightness of eye, a keenness of scent; they still were alert before action, quick, happy, present-minded; they ate to serve a practical need rather than any refinement of taste; and they had the buoyancy of fair prospects and noble promise—perhaps even the fine carelessness of assured winners when in the last lap sighting the goal.

They had halted on the col at 9.10 p.m. or a little later. Not too many hours remained to reach the summit and descend before dark. But enough, oh yes, enough; they were well agreed on that point. If they kept going the result was not in question. And what doubt they would keep on? The alternative, however, was suggested among them—the descent by the Corridor; a prospect clearly of ignoble ease, but quite seriously suggested on account of the weakest member. Shame couldn't have allowed him to accept such a proposal. They had trusted him so much! He was proud to be there, he would be proud to the end. They must trust him for the rest.

After forty minutes they were moving on again towards the Mur de la Cite. The great dome of Mont Blanc was fairly fronting them at last, theirs to win with stout hearts in a fair white field. But he no longer felt as they went forward the full zest of struggle. The way was easy; and he was confident of strength now, for the poison had lost its power and he had eaten food. The end was too certain. He was calm and a little sceptical. He began to fear an anticlimax, a disappointment in things attained. Wasn't it like a slice of bread and jam, the last unjammed portion? Wasn't the adventure ended and this merely a depressing fatigue? But in the mere act of firmly lancing the feet he found an answer to that last doubt; at each step upward and steeper there throbbed a dim faith refuting the heresy. The spirit didn't come so far to slip all down to nothing; all parts of such experience were significant; the dream stretched to the very end.

A breeze cool and bracing seemed to gather force as they plodded up the long slopes, more gentle now as they approached the final goal. He felt the wind about him with its old strange music. His thoughts became less conscious, less continuous. Rather than thinking or feeling he was simply listening—listening for distant voices scarcely articulate…. The solemn dome resting on those marvellous buttresses, fine and firm above all its chasms of ice, its towers and crags; a place where desires point and aspirations end; very, very high and lovely, long-suffering and wise…. *Experience*, slowly and wonderfully filtered; at the last a purged remainder…. And what is that? What more than the infinite knowledge that it is all worthwhile—all one strives for? How to get the best of it all? One must conquer, achieve, get to the top; one must know the end to be convinced that one can win the end—to know there's no dream that mustn't be dared…. Is this the summit, crowning the day? How cool and quiet! We're not exultant; but delighted, joyful; soberly astonished…. Have we vanquished an enemy? None but ourselves. Have we gained success? That word means nothing here. Have we won a kingdom? No… and yes. We have achieved an ultimate satisfaction… fulfilled a destiny…. To struggle and to understand never this last without the other; such is the law…. We've only been obeying an old law then? Ah, but it's *the* law… and we understand a little more. So ancient, wise and terrible—and yet kind we see them; with steps for children's feet.

* * *

Published as 'Mont Blanc from the Col du Géant by the Eastern Buttress of Mont Maudit' *Alpine Journal*, 1918 Vol. 32 pp 148ff.

4

RADIANT FROST
Mont Blanc, 1919

Picture four men bounding across Paris in what may be called a super-taxi. An animated discussion was proceeding between three of them, to the complete stupefaction of the fourth, who seemed to regard his companions as eccentrics beyond all hope, perhaps quite insane—but what else could he expect? Above the comical fat face of this bewildered individual immodest capitals in gold round his official cap announced 'Cox's Agency'. His business was to ship the three tourists across Paris. That the gentlemen who had reserved seats in the train to Grenoble should now be arguing as to whether after all they wouldn't take the train to Chamonix—it was impossible, *fantastique*. Nevertheless, the train to Chamonix, when they reached the Gare de Lyon, looked a nice train, and the three resolved to take it.

This irresponsible proceeding which threw to the winds, despite my protests, the deep-laid plans matured during the summer, took place on the evening of 28 July 1919. On the following morning, coming up the valley towards St Gervais, we were feasting our eyes on snow mountains. It was seven years since I had seen the Alps. To me they were a vision startlingly fresh and new—new as when I first saw them, and so overwhelmingly greater than the images I had conjured up that I seemed never to have seen them before. I realised that a thread of experience had been broken. I hardly connected what I saw now with what I had seen before. My mind was void of comparisons and particulars. I was starting again from the threshold; my mind was open like a child's to receive what it could. Whatever we might achieve, and we were wholly without plans, all would be adventure, vivid, surprising, delightful.

But however enchanting this new world seemed to me, I inevitably referred my observations to the intention of climbing peaks. The whole of the Mont Blanc group looked remarkably white; the snow was not of yesterday. The steep side of the Aiguilles was not plastered, but arêtes and ledges were everywhere piled with it; great quantities had peeled off, but elsewhere the even couches were dazzlingly white. Even on the West side of the valley large patches under the escarpments showed how little the winter snow had melted, and perhaps there was more snow to come now. The upper sky was hazy with fish-like clouds, and lower clouds were blowing up from the South and gathering upon the summits. The valley was hot and stuffy. We were hardly half-way up the path to Montanvert when a storm appeared to be on the point of bursting; but it was dissipated somehow or another and passed with no more spite than a few casual drops. I emphasise the phenomenon as one typical of the season. Till the middle of August when I left the Alps the weather always appeared to be unsettled; but it was always merciful. A midday haze, rather than cloud, repeatedly obscured the peaks and thickened perceptibly until about the hour of sunset. The nights were commonly much warmer than is usual in fine weather. However, local prophecy was always optimistic and it was always right.

I now come to the sober history of our mountaineering activities. We decided to spend the first day on the Requin. Having regard to the snow there was nothing else to be done except the Moine, which hadn't a vote.

It is not to be supposed of this party that they said confidently among themselves 'We will do the Requin'. One of us pointed out with admirable fortitude that it would be wholly unreasonable, on a first day, to rise before 6 a.m.; and his determined attitude easily carried the day. Accordingly, a formula was adopted acceptable to all consciences, 'We will go and look at the Requin.'

The looking took place next day chiefly during the breakfast hour. We had successfully found a way near the Trélaporte side of the glacier, and turned the corner so as to see the farther side of that remarkable arête of which the Requin is the final sentinel before it leaps down towards the Glacier du Géant. The problem which now confronted us, since it was already 8.15 a.m., and the night in any case had been too warm, was to avoid an arduous snow trudge up the Glacier du Plan, which would necessarily be our fate if we followed the usual route. Being quite untempted by Guido Mayer's route (Kurz, p.174) two courses were open to us; we could either attempt to follow G.W. Young's party (with Joseph Knubel, etc., see Kurz, p.173), climbing the S. arête in its entirety, or join this arête above its abrupt extremity by working up a small tributary glacier (see Kurz, p.173). The second alternative was chosen. We ascended in the direction of a well-marked couloir, descending from a point apparently in the middle of the S.E. face of our peak. This face was for the most part clear of snow, for the very good reason that all such superfluities had been shot down its steep wall on to the very slopes where our route lay. The prospects were good enough once we got there. But knee-deep snow on a first day is a formidable obstacle, and when the snow reaches half-way up the thigh—but I won't attempt to describe our agonies. It was about 11.30 a.m. when we took to the rocks on our left, above a shoulder where the subsidiary arête to the S. of us, as we mounted the snow, abutted the mountain. Porter led us swiftly on the rocks, and bearing always slightly to the left we reached the S. arête at 12.45 p.m. The prospects at this point were not rosy. It would be unreasonable to allow less than an hour and a half from the Épaule to the summit, and between us and that preliminary goal lay a considerable stretch of rocks, formidable by their steepness and crowned by the Chapeau, a most unpleasant-looking obstacle. Porter apparently was the fittest of the party and capable of much; of Elliott's state no more need be said than that in the secondary contest with his particular enemy, *mal de montagne,* his head, like Henley's, was 'bloody' but still 'unbowed'. My own physical condition was somewhere between these two. If I could flatter myself in more optimistic moments by computing that in one direction I could do not much less than Porter, I was ready to admit, after anything like a struggle, that I might be capable in the other direction of no less than Elliott.

With our varying estimates of the task before us we proceeded at 1.15 to ascend the arête. I confess that I allowed my imagination to suppose that, if all, things worked together for our success, we might conceivably reach the Épaule by, say, 2.45, and reach the summit, if we decided to go on, at 4 o'clock, or in any case descend by the usual route to the Glacier du Plan. The arête at all events would present no impassable gendarmes; it was simply the unserrated upper edge of a great tooth slightly inclined, where we were, from the perpendicular. Our pace, however, was not very rapid. It was necessary almost everywhere to climb one at a time, and, if convenient chimneys were found breaking the steep wall, they were not all to be climbed without some consideration, nor, one or two of them, without notable fatigue. My optimistic allowance of time to the Épaule must have been almost consumed when we reached the base of the Chapeau. Perhaps there was no point in going on. But for my part, I had an invincible desire to reach the crest beyond the Chapeau and look down on the other side. Porter's good nature was willing to gratify my curiosity, and we both counted on Elliott's stout heart. Under these somewhat whimsical circumstances, for it was clear enough now that we could not reach the summit, Porter proceeded to climb a crack in a steep slab, executed a delicate traverse to the right, and somehow managed to convey himself straddle-legged up a smooth edge of granite to a platform. It was a 40-ft lead of great difficulty, a truly remarkable exploit at that late period in a strenuous first day. Another half-hour of difficult snow and rock work was required to reach the crest.

It was now 8.45 p.m. The Épaule was still half an hour, perhaps an hour, farther along the arête, even had we contemplated a descent onto an unknown glacier. Our course was obvious; we retraced our steps. We were off the rocks at 6.30 p.m., and reached Montanvert with the last light.

31 July It was two days later when we started forth again, this time for the Col du Géant. We had rested luxuriously after our look at the Requin; the mountains at the head of the glacier were still in a dangerous state, as were the Verte and the Dru, and nothing tempted us on that side. But it was thought that we might perhaps accomplish some part of the arête between the Aiguille du Géant and the Calotte de Rochfort.

The walk from Montanvert to the Col du Géant is not an expedition to be lightly undertaken—or not at all events by a party still unfit. Above the ice-fall one may expect more labour than excitement, and if he is late there the labour may be excessive. On the other hand, to be there betimes demands a bout of crevasse-leaping in the dark. While so much snow was still unhardened on the glacier, and when the nights were so unsatisfactorily warm, the prospect of a heavy snow grind was a prime consideration. We started, however, no earlier than 3.30 a.m. in the expectation that the first glimmer of daylight would help us up the glacier, and with the hope that we might yet be early enough to find hard snow above the ice-fall. Our calculation was justified on the first head; when we found ourselves about 4.30 a.m. happily past the corner, in the middle of the glacier and approaching the ice-fall, we were well satisfied with our performance. But what were the prospects: we were walk-

ing on snow, firm enough it is true; but where was the crisp suggestion of frost? Allowing for a colder temperature higher up we
could still be certain, if we followed the usual route, that we should
trudge soft snow in plenty.

I hope that it was more in adventure than in laziness that we
resolved to circumvent what Nature proposed. It was a favourable
occasion to try experiments on a glacier, and the E side of the ice-
fall was not uninviting, by reason of a plausible trough which sepa-
rates the more broken part of it from the lower rocks of La Noire.
There was everything to be gained by this course if it would go; the
W.-facing slopes above and beyond would be little affected by the
sun, if we could but reach them soon enough, and we should have
a shorter line to the Col du Géant. Those who are confronted by
the deep blue sea turn to the Devil and hope for the best. Such was
our optimism on the present occasion. The Devil at least is as an
unknown quantity; his lure is caprice and he may make a mistake.

To describe in detail the sequel to our decision is a task which I
trust will not be expected of me. Of all the mountaineering adver-
saries which a mountaineer may meet, the most surprising,
resourceful, attractive, the gamest when he chooses to fight, is,
beyond question, a big glacier. But the contest is indescribable. A
climber who takes a short cut on a glacier can but look at his watch
and count the lost hours. I can only relate of this adventure that our
experiences were not unusual. We did not on the frail edge of sore
blue cold pinnacle, too elegant to be sound, run the risk of being
engulfed along with it. Nor did we hew steps tediously up any perpendicular wall of formidable dimensions. But the way was exciting
enough—first on the right of the trough, then in the middle of it,
and finally across a bergschrund to a little snow slope under the
rocks till we leaped from the ultimate tongue of La Noire to the
white fields beyond. Here the crust would hardly bear us; we
became full of devices to float upon it; we took quick little steps, we
leaned upon our axes, we dug in our toes and crooked knees

towards the slope, or painfully walked with boot soles turned out to press the thrust along the surface. At times we positively went upon all fours, the ubiquitous ice-axe playing spar to the shipwrecked. I believe we must have tried every manner of going that is swifter for a biped than to go upon his belly. Anything we found was better than to go through; in treading delicately we could have given lessons to Agag. The sun was always chasing us—a bright menace—and we fled like bats, remained almost constantly in shadow, and almost never floundered. It was not altogether a straight line that we followed, but it seemed as we went miraculously direct. The slope was such that for the best part of the distance we never could obtain a clear view ahead; the choice of line was speculative in the extreme. We had no knowledge as to where the crevasses lay; we could only guess. But though the crevasses, when we found them, were perturbingly immense, the Fates were always kind; some chasms which seemed to cut us off completely were found to be choked with helpful snow, others were cunningly bridged by frail arches of ice or just not too wide for a judicious leap. It was exciting, exhilarating, and sometimes hard work. Little time was lost. We met the tracks from the other side not far from Le Petit Flambeau and reached the col about midday, sufficiently weary and contentedly elated, as all should be who have avoided irksome labour and yet achieved their object.

1 August The next episode which I have to record is the saddest event short of disaster that can well happen to a party of mountaineers. From the moment that Elliott first mooted the proposal that we should come to Chamonix at once instead of Dauphiné an apprehension had always been present in our minds—that Elliott's knee would stop obstinately in the way like Balaam's ass. To criticise the vagaries of this remarkable joint would be unbecoming in anyone but its possessor. Suffice it to say, that for Alpine labour it has been usually brought to a benevolent disposition by a careful course of previous suggestion. But the couloirs of a government office during the summer months last year had contrariwise been a training in idleness. By the completion of our first expeditions it was brought to a state of open rebellion. It jibbed on the Requin, it creaked on the Glacier du Géant, and now was groaning vigorously on the Col. By evening it was evident that it refused to be cajoled. Elliott, who alone could gauge his hurt, told us plainly what it meant. At the least a week's complete rest was needed to restore his knee; it was unlikely to be fit even then for serious climbing. The only wisdom was to return to England at once.

It was a strange contrast next morning on that little high plateau so splendidly set, between the clear, vivid, hopeful, dawn calmly glorifying the peaks—a perfect morning on the one hand—and on the other a despairing party, setting forth not to win new summits, but to reach Montanvert in time for déjeuner and the train for Chamonix. We pottered for a time along the arête leading to La Tour Ronde to see the unparalleled beauty of Mont Blanc, and then mournfully, and very painfully I fear for Elliott, followed the tracks down the glacier.

The Trélaporte face of the Charmoz had attracted our attention on the way to the Col du Géant. I had wondered where exactly Joseph Pollinger had led his party so long ago as 1899. It was pointed out that wherever it was the route had been damned by Kurz as '*une des plus pierreuses*'. But this judgement I found incredible. Why should any place on that excessively steep face of hard granite be exposed to abnormal danger from falling stones? Stones might have fallen on the day of Pollinger's ascent, but were stones constantly falling there, or more frequently than in a hundred other places, on routes sanctified by venerable names and the common usage of climbers, where rocks were far more brittle and more disintegrated? The only way, we had agreed, to resolve this perplexity was to go and see. 'And why not?' I said to myself as I mounted the path. 'If ever two men are a better party than three it is on a steep rock face.

And if we succeed we shall get a bit of our own back.'

When it happens to him who bears the lantern that he loses his balance irrecoverably, with the result that the lantern is dashed against a rock and extinguished while the palm of his hand receives an ugly gash—when ruffled by one or two such small adventures it is difficult to believe that all is going well. Accordingly, my mood on the morning of 2 August, as we contoured the lower slopes of the E. arête of the Charmoz, was not perfectly optimistic. My right hand though sore enough was still serviceable, but I regretted a portion of skin unfortunately removed from an important finger-tip. Porter had already been critical of my lead, in his gentle manner (probably with justice); I was supposed to be conducting the party by the light of previous experience, and I was particularly anxious to find a good way. But our line was evidently too high; we became involved with difficult rocks, and were forced to struggle up a most unpleasant pitch when we ought to have been walking on easy ledges. The Glacier de Trélaporte presented no difficulties when we reached it, but it was annoying to observe that we should have done much better to make for an obvious notch only a few feet above it by ascending a snow couloir on the other side. It was annoying, too, that the slope was just so steep that it was necessary to chip steps for some distance up the glacier. We sat down at length for breakfast about 5.40 a.m. on some rocks immediately below the bergschrund, not much later than I had expected. But it still seemed a vaguely unsatisfactory expedition when we went on again. We were lucky to find the bergschrund passable at the right-hand corner. I remembered that G.W. Young's party, when they climbed the Grépon, had some difficulty at this point. But generally speaking, difficulties were not to be expected on this lower part. We were following the line towards the conspicuous Red Tower followed by all previous parties on this face. I had once been so far as that level myself and remembered no formidable obstacle. However, we soon found ourselves cutting steps above the bergschrund towards the rocks away on our left with no little labour, on account of three deep grooves whose sides were both steep and hard. We took fifty minutes from our breakfast place to the rocks. Hereabouts I knew that one should traverse away to the left; but the slab which presented itself for this purpose looked singularly uninviting. I wasted twenty minutes climbing a steep wall, and defeated here, attacked the slab below; the roughness of the rock made it an easier passage than it looked. We proceeded without hesitation after this, bearing slightly to the left, until we found ourselves at a corner where a buttress abuts a wall; we were separated from some chimneys away on our right by a patch of deep snow. The obvious plan was to make at once for these chimneys, as Porter recommended. But my judgement was affected by vague recollections. I was tempted to make a reconnaissance in the other direction, and there unfortunately I saw sitting on a ledge a large friendly cairn. I became possessed of the obstinate conviction that the wall above should be climbed and not the chimneys. Two somewhat desperate and futile attempts led to further waste of time, until eventually we crossed to the chimneys, which were found to go easily enough and led to the bay, a marked feature of the mountain, at the level of the Red Tower. It was now 8.30 a.m. Porter, who was carrying most of our burden, had been wonderfully patient behind an errant leader. But I was ill-satisfied. There had been no fizz about our performance, and while one may forgive hesitations and futilities when the obstacles are really formidable, he desires the preliminaries of an expedition such as this to go with a click.

From the point we had now reached much could be seen. The face of the Grépon presented its grim bare slabs in continuation of the line we had followed. Away to the right, on the other side of the bay, were the S.-facing rocks of the Charmoz E. arête, and most conspicuously the Aiguille de la République. The nick behind this elegant spike offers no attractions as a line of attack for the Charmoz. The problem is to reach the arête, where it assumes a comparatively horizontal habit above this step. The topography of all the country which now lay within our immediate view was related, as we saw it, to one central feature, a couloir of which the origin was concealed, but which descended towards us, apparently from the direction of the Charmoz; the Grépon was its true right wall in this lower part. Its true left wall was a conspicuous rib, a high buttress of the arête in question and leading exactly to the point which we wanted to gain above the Aiguille de la République.

Our objective, therefore, was perfectly clear and we had little doubt that it had also been Pollinger's. The only doubt remaining was how and where to join our rib. Its extremity was a forbidding red wall, perhaps a hundred metres above us. The gully might prove the best way round, and at all events deserved inspection. Not many minutes were spent in determining our plan before we moved upwards again, on smooth but broken plaques. It became evident as we approached the gully that its condition, if not its nature, was sufficiently repulsive; we had no wish to contend against a vigorous young torrent in a smooth open groove, nor to go up where whatever was so inclined would be coming down—not unless we were obliged. A convenient traverse led back to the right of the red wall above us; and we halted twenty minutes for a prune and a pipe. The next two hundred feet contained no obstacle of supreme difficulty; but with snow on sloping ledges and an angle that permitted no liberties, it was an exacting pitch, and we found the hour 10.30 a.m. when we reached the narrow crest of our rib above its first formidable obstacle.

It is idle perhaps to analyse those swift changes of mood or sensation which are the common experience of mountaineers. They may come to us at any time through some incident in our adventure, through altering circumstances of our progress, or merely from the fact of a halt when we come together and review our situation.

We paused only, and looked upwards; and I became aware that the whole face of things, for me at all events, had completely changed. I saw by Porter's expression that it had changed for him too. His smile had too much enjoyment to be grim, and was too serious for mere amusement. We looked up at the ferocious crags, and felt, I imagine, as a hunter feels when he gets sight of his tiger. I have in mind an optimistic hunter; for we were certainly elated. And yet we had not too much to be happy about. In four hours we had made perhaps 1500 feet from the bergschrund. We computed nearly as much again to the summit, and the great difficulties were all in front of us.

A few steps above us the buttress was notched, before rising again in an obstacle no less abrupt than the red wall which we had outflanked. We turned towards the gully and found a chimney. It was necessary to push up through a hole behind a chockstone—a tiring struggle, because the hole was iced, and while cutting out a way much care had to be taken to avoid bringing down too large a flake. From the shallow cave above the chockstone direct progress was strictly barred. The left wall offered the only hope. Luckily it was possible for the second to give a shoulder, so that the leader could be thrust over the edge on to a sloping slab above. It was an unpleasant position standing there with no particular handhold, but for the encouragement of an excellent belay. A minute crack running vertically up the slab alone seemed to break its even surface. Luckily the point of the axe could be inserted; by turning the shaft over to the left and keeping the point pressed in it could be sufficiently secured; the left hand in this way did the required pulling, while the right fingers prevented a slip. Without an axe it would have been impossible to get up this slab, in height about 20 feet. The second dexterously availed himself of a stirrup-rope, which was just long enough to be within his grasp for the first struggle. We were still, as it were, in the middle of a pitch, but there was now a choice of alternative routes, of which the leader chose the worse. After ascending vertical flakes he had again to surmount a difficult slab when some distance above support. The second bore his burden up a chimney having a less malicious disposition, which proved moderately tractable after a difficult start.

My next recollection after these salient events, which I see quite clearly engraved in my mind with the familiar characters of nervous tension, is of issuing from some sort of groove which we had followed without difficulty above the chimney last mentioned. We now found ourselves once again on the crest of our buttress, followed a ledge to the right, and saw above us on this side a deeply-cut chimney, or subsidiary gully it might almost be called. Beyond the fact that we accepted what was offered with grateful hearts and some little show of enthusiasm, neither Porter nor myself could recall even a few hours later precisely what happened next. We agreed that it was, like Prospero's island, a wholesome place, where the air breathed upon us sweetly; the rocks were steep and sound as one could wish to find them; the wedged axe was useful more than once, and strenuous but not desperate exertion was required. Buoyed by confidence in Nature which had been so kind to us, happy, optimistic, we proceeded swiftly for about 200 feet. Even the final pitch, partially iced, a steep wall with very small holes—a difficulty we reckoned of the first order—detained us only for a few minutes, and when at 1.15 we gained a platform once more on the edge of the rib we were now proud of our progress. Here we halted for lunch.

The reflections engendered on this high perch were for the most part comforting: but two little doubts cast perceptible shadows. The sky was clouding over and mist was gathering about the peaks. A sphinx, presumably one of the Charmoz summits, could be discerned, when we looked round the corner of the gully, coldly regarding us; but suddenly we could no longer see it. Neither of us much believed, after the past few days, in the malice of this omen. But even an innocent mist was undesirable if we were to find our way down by a route unknown to us. The second doubt was perhaps more serious. Kurz's account of Pollinger's ascent makes mention of a 6-7 metre chimney. Why then was nothing said of the remarkable chimney we had just come up? Could 6-7 be a misprint for 60-70? Such an explanation was far from satisfying us. Had Pollinger, in fact, ever been where we were? Kurz said not even so much as that his party had ascended a steep buttress; on the contrary, he spoke of a gully. The more one thought about it, the more clear it became that we had not followed the line of the first ascent. Whatever peace of mind may be drawn from the assurance that a man has been there before you could be ours no longer. What lay between us and our goal? And would it go? We judged that the distance could not now be great. We should soon know the issue. Such thoughts if they gave ground for some anxiety were chiefly exhilarating, entirely undepressing, and served, as did the sombre shadow of a cloud, to hasten our steps.

Immediately above us the rocks sloped back more gently than before. My pipe was scarcely well alight when we went on straight ahead. We had proceeded perhaps 150 feet when I knocked it sideways against a rock and out of my mouth; it slithered down snow, past Porter, apparently doomed and then by some miraculous good fortune turned a somersault, took a header, and stopped. Porter, roused to sympathy by my cry of anguish, made no hesitation in unroping himself and quickly recovered my precious pipe. It was a good omen, but also a warning. The rocks were getting steeper—steeper than they had appeared from our luncheon place—and a little higher I now saw were probably impracticable. We chose the obvious alternative, and mounted snow on our right into a gully continuing our previous line. The first pitch pulled us up. We had reckoned with rocks but not with ice, and I feared delay. It was necessary to set to work with the axe, chipping awkwardly with the left hand from a strained position. The issue hung on one small step cut in the frailest imaginable structure just clinging to the rock. From this it was necessary somehow to pull oneself over the awkward bulge above it. The obstacle was the most obstinate we had yet encountered—the sort, where a man sticks and decides that he can't, but, knowing he must, continues wriggling till he does.

We came forth finally from this second story of our great chimney or little gully to find a change of circumstances, showing that the end was near. The buttress had narrowed almost to a knife-edge, as a good buttress should, before the point of abutment. Its structure was becoming fantastic, and even was showing a dangerous tendency to indulge in superfluous ornament. Some curiously devised overhangs and angular projections in the first 20 feet above a narrow gap invited strange contortions in the climber; but we were too excited to contort ourselves for long; this obstacle was carried with a rush—in so far as that expression may be suitable to the balanced performances of mountaineers. We quickly mounted the beast's back beyond in the expectation of seeing the end. We were not, in one respect, disappointed. Whatever we saw was probably the last of its kind, and it appeared to mark the limit of our day's adventure. Separated from us by a square-cut gap was a gendarme about 100 feet high—it was no fantastic shape prancing upon the edge of space, but a solemn and utterly forbidding sentry with his back to the wall. We were faced by an obstacle unassailable. On the right vicious slabs swept down to the Aiguille de la République; by traversing across the head of them it might be possible to reach a farther wall apparently near the junction of the buttress with the arête. Porter thought this quite without hope; it could be the hope only of desperate men. It seemed to me just conceivable that a way might be found on that side, but the demand of nerve and strength would obviously be so great that I doubted whether we should be justified in launching the assault at so late a stage in our day's hard work. To the left the situation appeared still more hopeless. The gully on that side had now opened into a bay; towards this the rocks fell away with appalling steepness, while the tower itself capped the precipice with an overhang. And beyond this, on the arête of the Charmoz, now so near, I noted a perpendicular wall some 30 feet high, which might be impassable should we gain the arête.

With all my optimism blown away like smoke I climbed down into the gap, and proceeded to traverse carefully to the left side towards the overhang. At least, I thought, I will look round the corner. My curiosity was gratified by a ray of hope. Here was a little bay perched above the precipice; it might be possible to get up the farther side of it. The entrance was difficult, but I managed to crawl under the overhang and land my knees on to a sloping slab. On the farther side I climbed in a corner up to a mantelshelf on my left. Above this was a short wall. It was evidently very difficult, and I couldn't tell whether it would go. I sent back a depressing account to Porter. My confidence was at a low ebb, but his reply showed that he possessed, or he assumed, the glorious gift of blind faith. It was necessary in any case for him to move, for I should want more rope if I was to make the attempt. Happily I was able to take up a position so as to press him inwards as he passed the overhang, and help his arrival on to the sloping slab which the rucksack might otherwise have rendered extremely awkward; and by similar means I calculated we should be able to return. On the farther side of the recess was a patch of snow. Here Porter drove in his axe. It was not a sufficient protection, but it might serve, and it was the best available. If he had wavered at this point I doubt if I could have tackled the pitch. I mounted again in the right-angled corner and traversed out leftwards on to the mantelshelf. I was now almost directly above my second, and above me was a wall as nearly as possible perpendicular—a short obstacle—only some 15 to 20 feet high, but, I confess, an alarming one. I was conscious during a few seconds' hesitation of confused reflections, proceeding from the thought that but a short time before I had been in the mood to tackle such a pitch with a gesture of confident enjoyment, with the élan of a leader leading to victory. Now it was different; the spirit was unwilling. Was the flesh any weaker for that, I wondered, or if more effort of will is required to start, is there less effort available to get up? I looked down with a backward, uncomfortable glance, to see Porter in the most workmanlike fashion belaying the rope round his axe in which neither of us felt security. I positively disliked him for his imperturbability. Still, there he was, imperturbable, efficiently cheerful, a moral fact from which I saw no escape. I looked away from him, half in anger that he should combine so much genial amiability— more than usual—and so much veteran's righteousness round his damned belay; half in sorrow that any such fool could be found as to enjoy, apparently, our present situation; and at the same time, as I looked upward again, in some further strata of consciousness I was amusedly delighted that Porter was playing the game so well.

As to the difficulty of what followed I feel singularly incompetent to pronounce judgement. The steep little wall was climbed, safely, as it had to be; but the fingerholds, seemed distressingly small, and it was necessary to change feet on a minute foothold. Balance, no doubt, was chiefly required; perhaps it was not a particularly difficult pitch. Porter followed more easily than I had expected. However, my memory is left with the picture of a short intense effort of mind and body in a situation as exposed as I care for.

I had imagined once this wall was climbed that we should find a way up, one way or another, on this side of our arête, and I was disappointed after ascending a few feet higher to perceive that we could not proceed in that line. Porter, however, made a good lead up to the right, and by means of a slanting crack rejoined the arête. The great obstacle had been surmounted, but we withheld our cheers. Our hopes were not yet certainty. I had to take a shoulder to mount the next step in the arête, raced up 50 feet, crossed a gendarme, reached a farther point, and then shouted to Harold to follow. As he came up stepping off his axe and by some ingenuity recovering it, I was seated on the final pinnacle, duly placed to crown our buttress, and looking away over the arête and down to friendly Montanvert.

We were now divided from the summit ridge of the Charmoz by a sharp snow arête interspersed by a few rocky obstacles. With feet dug in on the Montanvert side and arms over the crest, we worked quickly along to the first of these, the perpendicular wall I had already remarked. It was easily surmounted and our way was plain before us. The mountain no longer resisted; the day was ours. At 3.45 p.m. we joined the summit ridge.

The weather luckily had not been unkind. Cloud was blowing on and off our peak; but not so as to enshroud us thickly. And in any case we could have followed tracks in snow, as we soon proceeded to do. An uneventful descent took us back to our abode at the due hour, in time for dinner.

A few words must be added in retrospect about our climb on the Charmoz. For persons hardly fit and certainly not yet hard it was a sufficiently strenuous day. But it was a proper expedition for two guideless climbers. They simply rubbed their noses against the rocks, and if they could not have climbed these rocks safely they would have retired. The only risks taken were in descending by the usual way, over the Nantillons Glacier. The ascent was never exposed to falling stones. A third man would necessarily have caused delay at several places, and a party of more than two will never, I expect, have much time to spare on this route. It is true that we wasted about forty-five minutes below the Red Tower, and it would have been possible to have saved the twenty minutes' halt which we took at 9.30. Possibly the presence of ice in several places cost us another forty-five minutes, but we were early on the glacier, and I don't think our pace was slow; from the time we reached the bottom of the long chimney, and particularly after lunch, it was as fast as I have ever travelled on difficult rocks. We had time to spare no doubt for the descent. Personally, I have a respect for the Nantillons Glacier. I would always like to pass the séracs before sunset—after the westerly sun has done its worst and before the critical hour or so when frost sets in for the night.

I have described this expedition at some length for purely literary reasons. It is possible to indicate the nature of an expedition quite briefly. But I confess I have not the art of making a story without some details, and to make a story seemed the best chance of interesting you.

The incidents of rock-climbing usually afford more material for description than hours spent on snow and ice; there are notable exceptions, such as Mummery's ascent of the Col du Lion and our late President's ascent of Mont Blanc by the Peuteret arête; but I think it will generally be found that much more ink has been used in describing difficulties on rocks than those on ice and snow. From my point of view this is regrettable. For the best that climbing can give us, variety is needed; but ice and snow seem to me to afford finer experiences than rocks. I should be inclined to accept as an expression of the first mountaineering instinct Shelley's simple words, 'I love snow and all the radiant forms of Frost.' I don't love an Alpine peak devoid of snow. I hate the Dolomites, for instance, though I have never seen them, for their sterile aridity which no photograph can conceal; they seem to me an unquiet sort of desert. I envy no mountaineer so much as those who made the Brenva ascent when it was still comparatively safe; and it seems paradoxical that I should have been at pains to describe an expedition that contains so little of what I consider the finer element.

This attitude may seem ungenerous. But I don't deny the delights of the Charmoz, and I hope I am grateful for them. The Aiguilles are deservedly attractive. They have an indefinable quality of good breeding. Fishermen say of the salmon, I am told, that he is a gentleman—he refuses to give himself meekly away; he plays up till the last; he has the quality. The Aiguilles are not so much gentlemen as ladies. Porter and I were agreed that our Aiguille behaved with admirable spirit. To complete the tale I set forth to tell, I have still to make reference to two expeditions, though I shall not describe them.

Interest in the nature of our enjoyment of the Alps is concerned not only with particular peaks, but with the campaign as a whole. To those who find themselves in Chamonix wishing to be on the Col du Géant, it may seem desirable for the sake of the campaign to take a peak on the way; or they may merely wish to avoid repetition of a snow trudge they know too well. The latter was our case, and we planned to reach the Col du Géant, excluding the greater part of a toilsome walk, by traversing the Aiguille du Midi from the Plan de l'Aiguille. It was perhaps mere laziness, but the enterprise was not without point, for it appeared from Kurz that no satisfactory ascent of the Midi had been made on this side. So far as I know only two parties have recorded expeditions here—the first, Mr Dent's party in 1899 reached the N.E. arête in bad weather, and descended hastily on the far side without reaching the summit rocks; at all events they made the first ascent of this face. The second party, Mlle Engster with a guide and two porters, were less successful.

Both parties used the great couloir which comes down from near the summit. Whether this was altogether a wise proceeding I have not sufficient knowledge to judge. One would certainly expect it to be a safe line of ascent in normal conditions, but to descend it late in the day when the sun has come round (it faces W.) is a very different proposition, and a party ascending this face must reckon with the possibility of defeat higher up, where the cutting might be very arduous or either of two obstacles impassable.

The line chosen by Porter and myself is to the left of this one all the way. Crampons were used in the couloir—we should have required steps without them. The rocks in the middle section were easy. The general angle of the hanging glacier and snow slopes above is decidedly steep. We kept to the edge as far as possible, and thus avoided any slopes of bare ice on either hand. There were difficulties in only two places, firstly, in crossing the bergschrund, which appeared possible at only one point. It was necessary to get up a crack in an ice-wall. Secondly, where the final ice-wall meets the rocks, which were partially iced. This proved extremely difficult.

It was late, 12.15, when we reached the top of this peak; and the weather looked really bad. Nevertheless, I have little doubt we committed an error of judgement in deciding to descend to Montanvert; various considerations came in; we reckoned we shouldn't be fit for a long climb next day, and at the hotel we should find letters. In any case, we took the wrong line, though it was also Mr Dent's, making for the Rognon, near the ice-fall of the Géant Glacier. It was a very laborious descent in deep soft snow till we reached the tracks on the Glacier de Plan coming from the Requin.

We found ourselves eventually at the Rifugio Torino contemplating a reconnaissance on Mont Blanc. I was not happy about the prospects, and found myself awake at intervals during the night going over again in my mind the arguments for and against this expedition. Was it really a suitable expedition for a party of two? And for this party? And there constantly recurred the vision of a certain bleak edge of snow, or it might be ice, where we had seen powdered snow whisked in a fierce tourbillon such as might blow a party off the mountain. The wind was moaning during the night, and was still unquiet when we were called. Porter exhibited a tendency to wait for more propitious signs. But an interval of silence was followed by gentle snoring, and it was impossible to believe his judgement to proceed from a clear, unbiased mental process. The question as to whether we ought to start became involved in another—what would be good for Harold? The urgency of moral persuasion was now applied.

A little later we were treading the steps up to the col by lantern light. We had hardly popped our noses above the rim when we were furiously assaulted by an unseen enemy, whose first act of violence was to blow out our candle. You may remember that there is a hut less glorious than the Rifugio Torino situated at the level of the Col. Its emptiness was slightly cheered at that early hour before the dawn, by two pipes peacefully smoked and a conversation dim, solemn and fragmentary. The barbarian invasion, as it seemed, of Italy from the north did not cease; the hordes swept shuddering over the pass or fled screaming round the crags; and another project was born into the world. Below at the Rifugio two other Englishmen were presumably stirring towards resolved activities which they might already be half regretting. It was a favourable moment to try suggestion.

As a sequel to this thought, four men—the two others were Professor Pigou and Mr McLean—after lingering just so long as to know from its magic touch on peak after peak that the old fire was still alive, jogged down the steep path on the Italian side. Two of them at least had no passports, and to the interest of outwitting tracks on a moraine was to be added that of outwitting the gendarmerie. It was this thought, and the liberal advice of the inhabitants, when we were sitting in the shade at Purtud, after eating a breakfast worthy of that green oasis, that drove us from the alternative of passing there a day and a night. Those who have spent a hot summer's day, as hot as an August day can be—and have not started very early—in walking first up the Val Veni, and, farther, up the Miage Glacier, will appreciate the moral worth of our resolution. But I must admit that I found it a most enjoyable walk, and it was ultimately enlivened by circumstances which will remain unforgettable. Later in the afternoon of this same day the same four men might have been observed cutting steps up the Glacier du Mont Blanc on their way to the Quintino Sella hut, and with them, curiously enough, a fifth member to their party—a singularly passive member from all appearances, for he was frequently left sitting upon any convenient ledge and thereafter hauled up another stage, let down into a crevasse with a sickening swing, to be hoisted out on the farther side, and eventually pitched and pulled at the same time off the glacier altogether on to *terra firma*. This hapless personage was no less a burden than four small logs tied together at the end of our spare rope. The ascent to the Quintino Sella hut is steep—I doubt if any ascent to a hut is steeper—and the four weavers' beams arrived there that evening the least exhausted members of their party. There was wood enough already at the hut, as Professor Pigou had foretold; but his was merely that cynicism about the world as we find it which is born of present discomfort; the true critic might have asked what sort of a job it would be cutting and splitting those little logs for a fire, and how it might agree with the only tool available, somebody's ice-axe, which must never be mine.

On the following day we traversed Mont Blanc. We did not find it a difficult ascent—following, I imagine, more or less closely the line first chosen by Mr Kennedy. But it has rarely, if ever, been my fortune to spend a more agreeable day on the Alps—a day more than agreeable, a satisfying day. It is not altogether easy to account for this feeling. In the ordinary way I find a close correspondence between the intensity of the struggle and the keenness of enjoyment. In this case the real struggle had taken place on the previous day; in so far as mountaineering qualities were required for this expedition they were required chiefly for the ascent to the hut. Perhaps this fact was partially responsible for our enjoyment. The second day was a long, unchecked, and glorious reward for the first. Is there any other mountain, I wonder, where the first day counts for so much? I call to mind the approaches to various huts; and how few are worth recalling for any interest in their unpleasantness! Another cause suggests itself as contributing to this day's enjoyment. The companionship of tried friends on the mountains is undoubtedly a blessing but the converse is not true—that of untried friends need not always be a curse. A care for the brotherly relation has its uses, we are all agreed, in the mountaineering fraternity, but the discovery of a brother in the mountaineer can hardly be so interesting elsewhere, or so delightful, as upon the mountain side.

There is a further delight which I connect with this last expedition of my climbing season. The tentative advances and temporary defeats, hesitations and delays, linked together by a continuous persistence where the way is intricate and success is withheld for weary hours, or perhaps in the final decision—all that is a wonderful experience, and perhaps we like ourselves best for the efforts and endurance which the resistance of a great mountain demands. But easier successes have also their joys, and not the least of these is the mere rhythm of motion, the smooth, unchecked, harmonious advance of a party, where a great mountain offers from its abundance an infinite variety; though no remarkable skill may be required to surmount the obstacles, no little skill may be used to preserve that harmony, to achieve that intimate combination between the members of a party which is itself not only the most important of means, but a sufficient end and a sufficient delight.

And, finally, is not an ascent of Mont Blanc under any circumstances supremely satisfying? Or is this merely a hymn of praise to my mistress? I confess I have never walked up to the summit from the Grands Mulets; but I should be far from despising such an enterprise. A great mountain is always greater than we know: it has mysteries, surprises, hidden purposes; it holds always something in store for us. One need not go far to learn that Mont Blanc is *capable de tout*. It has greatness beyond our guessing—genius, if you like—that indefinable something about a mountain to which we know but one response, the spirit of adventure.

* * *

Read before the Alpine Club, 4 May 1920, published as 'Our 1919 Journey'

Alpine Journal, Vol. 33 pp 166ff

Everest

'The enormity of the task ahead.'
George Leigh Mallory

5

RECONNAISSANCE
Mount Everest, 1921

The reconnaissance of Mount Everest is a long story, and I do not propose to tell it now. It was necessary for our purpose, firstly, to seek in an unexplored country the most convenient approaches to various parts; secondly, by regarding the mountain from many different points of view to come to a correct understanding of its shape, and distinguish the vulnerable parts of its armour; finally, to pit our skill against the mountain wherever an opportunity of ascent presented itself. In the first two objects our task was largely accomplished between 23 June, when we set out from Tingri, and 18 August, when we first reached the Lhakpa La and looked over into the snow basin, which is the head of the East Rongbuk glacier. The final phase of the reconnaissance occupied the first three weeks of September, and I call it the 'Assault,' because we intended to climb as far up the mountain as we were able.

We had discovered before the final phase that the summit of Mount Everest was formed by the convergence of three arêtes. The faces which lay between them were clearly seen to be impracticable. The south arête is blocked by the south peak, a formidable crest about 28,000 feet high. The other two arêtes, west-north-west and north-east, are so steep in their lower parts that access is impossi-

ble. The only possible line of ascent is to reach the upper part of
the north-east arête from the north. Between Everest and the north
peak is a high snow col (about 23,000 feet), and it looks possible to
get up from here.

The line of approach chosen to this col had been determined by
a variety of circumstances, more particularly by the abundance of
fuel in the Kharta Valley which had suggested an advance from the
eastern side; but this approach would involve the crossing of another snow col, the Lhakpa La (22,500 feet), which we had already
reached. Once the snow was firm the way there would present no
difficulties.

It had become evident during our reconnaissance in July and
August that any serious climbing on the great mountain itself must
wait on the weather—if only for the sufficient reason that the
labour of carrying loads over unmelted snow would be an unen-
durable strain upon our coolies. Our plans were based upon the
assumption that what the wise men prophesied about the weather
would come true. We were promised a fine September. Some time
about the beginning of the month the monsoon would end, and
then we should have clear days of glorious sunshine and warmth to
melt the snow, and cold nights to freeze it; at worst the calm spell
would only be broken by a short anger. And so it was arranged in
hope, if not in confidence, to move up on the first signs of
improvement. Already, before we came down to Kharta, our
advanced base camp had been moved up. It was now situated at
about 17,300 feet on a convenient grassy plateau and only a reasonable stage below our 20,000 feet camp, where some light tents
and stores had also been left. At these two camps we had, in fact,
left everything which we should not absolutely require at Kharta, so
that few mountaineering stores would have to be carried up from
the base when we came up again. Our first task would be to supply
the advanced base with food and fuel, and a start had already been

Mallory, Wheeler, Bullock, Morshead, front. Wollaston, Howard-Bury, Heron, Roeburn, rear.

made by collecting here a pile of wood, nominally thirty loads. Transport in any case was not likely to be a difficulty in the early stages. Local coolies could easily be hired, and Colonel Howard-Bury was to follow us up after a short interval with all available strength to help in every possible way.

The first object which our plans must include was, of course, to reach the north col; by finding the way to this point we should establish a line of attack and complete a stage of our reconnaissance. Secondly, we must aim at reaching the north-east arête. In so far as it was an object of reconnaissance to determine whether it was possible to climb Mount Everest, our task could never be complete until we had actually climbed it; but short of that it was important to have a view of the final stage, and could we reach the great shoulder of the arête we should at least be in a better position to estimate what lay between there and the summit. Finally, we saw no reason to exclude the supreme object itself. It would involve no sacrifice of meaner ends; the best would not interfere with the good. For if it should turn out that the additional supplies required for a larger campaign were more than our coolies could carry, we could simply drop them and aim less high.

In organising the assault we had to consider how our camp could be established firstly at Lhakpa La, or, perhaps better, beyond it at a lower elevation, secondly at the north col, and finally as high as possible, somewhere under the shoulder, one thought, at about 26,500 feet. From the camp on the north col we should have to carry up ten loads, each of 15 lbs., which would provide tents enough and sleeping-sacks and food for a maximum of four sahibs and four coolies. Sixteen coolies were allowed for this task; twelve would, therefore, have to return on the day of their ascent and sleep at the north col; on the assumption that they would require an escort of sahibs, who must also sleep at this camp, four small tents must remain there, making six in all to be carried up to this point.

The lower end of the ladder must be so constructed as to support the weight at the top. It was comparatively a simple matter to provide the earlier camps. The first above the advanced base could be supplied before we moved up to sleep there, the coolies returning on the same day whenever they carried up loads. And the same plan could be adopted for the second at Lhakpa La; only one journey there, I calculated, would be required before we started from the 20,000-feet camp, and we could then go straight ahead without delay. The crux would lie in the stage from Lhakpa La to the north col. At the most we should have twenty-three coolies, sixteen who had been all along with the climbing party, three whom Wheeler had partially trained, and four more Sherpas, the maximum number being determined by the supply of boots. But it would not be necessary to carry on all the loads from Lhakpa La; and return journeys could be made from the north col, both by those who were not to stay there and by the twelve already mentioned who might fetch supplies if necessary on the final day of the assault. This plan was never executed in its later stages, and we cannot know for certain whether it would have held good. But it may be conjectured in view of our experience that the weakest link would have broken; either an extra day would have been spent between Lhakpa La and the north col, or, if we reached the north col, according to our programme, with the minimum of supplies, the coolies would not have been brought to this point a second time, and the climbing party would have been cut off from its reserves. And, granted the most favourable conditions for the attempt, in asking the coolies to carry loads of 30 lbs. on two consecutive days at these high altitudes we were probably expecting too much of them. It must be concluded, if this opinion is correct, that we had not sufficient coolies for what we intended.

On the last day of August, Bullock and myself were established once again at our advanced base. The weather had not yet cleared, though it was showing some signs of change. But it had been necessary to move up for the coolies' sake. At Kharta they had little to amuse them, and no work to employ their time; they were badly in need of a routine, which was easily enough provided. Besides, I wanted to be ready, and it seemed not too soon to begin carrying loads up to the next camp. There was no occasion for hurry in the event. We were obliged to wait nearly three weeks, until 19 September, before moving forward. The delay served no useful purpose. The work of supplying our present needs and providing for the future was sufficiently spread over the long tale of days, but interspersed with more rest and leisure than any one required. It was a blessing to be comparatively a large party. Howard-Bury and Wollaston and also Raeburn had come up on the 6th, Morshead and Wheeler on the 11th, and for two nights Heron was of our company.

We kept ourselves fit. But it amused nobody to watch the procession of clouds which precipitated sleet by day and snow by night, and our appetite for adventure could not be stimulated by the days of waiting in so dreary a scene.

When at last the weather cleared, it was evident that the fate of our enterprise would be decided by the sun's power to melt the snow. Before we left the advanced base I had good reason to expect that we should meet adverse conditions, and was so resolved at the same time that nothing was to be gained by waiting. The coolies were lightly laden up to the first advanced camp, and sufficiently unfatigued to proceed next day. On the 20th, therefore, leaving Bullock to accompany Wheeler, Morshead and I set forth to get fourteen loads up to Lhakpa La. We had one spare coolie who carried no load, and Sanglu, who was now our acting sirdar, four of us in all to break the trail for the loaded men. Snowshoes were not carried, because there were not enough to go round. Though our prospects of reaching a high point on Everest were already sufficiently dim, I intended to carry out the original plan until obliged by circumstances to modify it; it might prove necessary to spend an extra day in reaching the north col, and in that case we could perhaps afford to stop short of Lhakpa La and establish our camp below its final slopes. But if the strain on this first day was likely to be severe, I argued that the coolies could rest tomorrow, and that the second journey in frozen tracks would be easy enough. That on the col we should pass the night a few hundred feet higher (22,500 feet) was a relatively unimportant consideration. The great matter was to put heart into the coolies; it would be infinitely more encouraging to reach the crest with a sense of complete achievement, to see the clear prospect ahead, and to proceed downwards on the other side. Our start at an early hour on the 20th was sufficiently propitious. The night was exceedingly cold, and we walked on hard crisp snow up to the icefall. But the conditions here were no better than expected; higher they were worse than I had imagined possible. No firm steps could be stamped by the leaders to save the coolies behind, and each in turn had to contend with the shifting substance of fine powder. Three fell out in a state of exhaustion, and made their own way down. Two of the loads were bravely carried on until they had to be abandoned about 800 feet below the pass. The party straggled badly. But time was on our side, and gradually the eleven remaining loads arrived at their destination. The coolies had behaved in the gamest fashion, and no small share in the result was contributed by Morshead, who alternately plodded in front and kept together a party behind. Whatever measure of success we afterwards attained was secured on this day.

Now that we had obtained a clearer view of the north col it was possible to make more exact calculations, and it was evident we modify our plans. We had seen a wall of formidable dimensions, perhaps 1000 feet high; the surface was unpleasantly broken by insuperable bergschrunds, and the general angle was undoubtedly steep. The slopes of Everest to the south were out of the question, and if it were possible to avoid a direct assault by the north side the way here would be long, difficult, and exceedingly laborious. The wall itself offered the best chance, and I was in good hopes we could get up. But it would not be work for untrained men, and to have on the rope a number of laden coolies, more or less mountain-sick, conducted by so small a nucleus as three sahibs, who would also presumably be feeling the effects of altitude, was a proposition not to be contemplated for a moment. We must have as strong a party as possible, in the first place simply to reach the col and afterwards to bring up a camp, if we were able, as a separate operation. With this idea I selected the party. Wollaston could not be one of us as his place of duty was not with the van. Only Wheeler besides had sufficient mountaineering experience, and it was decided that he alone should accompany Bullock and myself on our first attempt to reach the col.

I had hoped we should have a full complement of coolies on the 22nd, but when morning came it was found that three, including two of the best men, were too ill to start; consequently some of the loads were rather heavier than I intended. But all arrived safely at Lhakpa La before midday. Visited by malicious gusts from the north-west the pass was cheerless and chilly. However, the rim afforded us some protection, and we decided to pitch our tents there rather than descend on the other side with the whole party, a move which I felt might jeopardise the return. I was not very happy about the prospects for the morrow. For my own part I had been excessively and unaccountably tired in coming up to the col; I observed no great sparkle of energy or enthusiasm among my companions. Sanglu was practically *hors de combat*; some of the coolies had, with difficulty, been brought up to the col and were more or less exhausted, and many complaints of headache, even from the best of them, were a bad sign.

There was no question of bustling off before dawn on the 23rd, but we rose early enough, as I supposed, to push on to the north col if we were sufficiently strong. Morshead and I, in a Mummery tent, had slept well. I congratulated myself on an act of mutilation in cutting two large slits in its roof. The rest had not fared so well, but seemed fit enough, and the wonderful prospect from our camp at sunrise was a cheering sight. With the coolies, however, the case was different. Those who had been unwell overnight had not recovered, and it was evident that only a comparatively small number would be able to come on. Eventually I gathered ten—two men, who both protested they were ill, casting lots for the last place; and of these ten it was evident that none were unaffected by the height, and several were more seriously mountain-sick.[4] Under these circumstances it was necessary to consider which loads should be carried on. Howard-Bury, Wollaston and Morshead suggested that they should go back at once so as not to burden the party with the extra weight of their belongings, and it seemed the wisest plan that they should return. Certain stores were left behind at Lhakpa La as reserve supplies for the climbing party. I decided at an early hour that our best chance was to take an easy day, and, after a late start and a very slow march, we pitched our tents on the open snow up towards the col.

It might have been supposed that in so deep a combe and sheltered on three sides by steep mountain slopes we should find a tranquil air and the soothing though chilly calm of undisturbed frost. Night came clearly indeed, with no gentle attentions. Fierce squalls of wind visited our tents and shook and worried them with the disagreeable threat of tearing them away from their moorings, and then scurried off, leaving us in wonder at the change and asking what next to expect. It was a cold wind at an altitude of over 22,000 feet, and however little one may have suffered the atmosphere discouraged sleep. Again, I believe I was more fortunate than my companions, but Bullock and Wheeler fared badly. Lack of sleep, since it makes one sleepy, always discourages an early start, and hot drinks take time to brew. In any case, it was wise not to start too soon so as to have the benefit of warm sun whenever our feet should be obliged to linger in cold snow or ice steps. It was an hour or so after sunrise when we started, and half an hour later we were breaking the crust on the first slopes under the wall. We had taken three coolies who were sufficiently fit and competent, and now proceeded to use them for the hardest work. Apart from one brief spell of cutting, when we passed the corner of a bergschrund, it was a matter of straightforward plugging, firstly slanting up to the right on partially frozen avalanche snow, and then left in one long upward traverse to the summit. Only one passage, shortly below the col, caused either anxiety or trouble. Here the snow was lying at a very steep angle and was deep enough to be disagreeable. About 500 steps of very hard work covered all the worst of the traverse, and we were on the col shortly before 11.30 a.m. By this time two coolies were distinctly tired, though by no means incapable of coming on; the third was comparatively fresh. Wheeler thought he might be good for another 500 feet, but had lost all feeling in his feet. Bullock was obviously tired, but by sheer will power would evidently come on—how far one could not say. For my part, I had had the wonderful good fortune of sleeping tolerably well at both high camps, and now I use this expression to denote, not a state of inter-

mittent vomiting, but simply one in which physical exertion
exhausts the body abnormally, and causes a remarkable disinclination to further exertion.

Finding my best form, I supposed I might be capable of another 2000 feet, and there would be no time for more. But what lay
ahead of us? My eyes had often strayed as we came up to the rounded edge above the col and the final rocks below the north-east arête.
If ever one had doubted whether the arête were accessible, it was
impossible to doubt any longer. On those easy rock and snow
slopes was neither danger nor difficulty. But at the present time
there was wind. Even where we stood under the lee of a little ice
cliff, it came in fierce gusts at frequent intervals, blowing up the
powdery snow in an evil manner sufficient to take one's breath away.
On the col beyond it was blowing a gale. And higher was a more
fearful sight. The powdery fresh snow on the great face of Everest
was being swept along in unbroken spindrift, and the very ridge
where our route lay was marked out to receive the full fury of this
onslaught. We could see the blown snow deflected upwards for a
moment where the wind met the ridge only to rush violently down
in a veritable blizzard on the leeward side. To see, in fact, was
enough; the wind had settled the question; it would have been folly
to go on. Nevertheless, we struggled a few steps further to put the
matter to the test. For a few moments we exposed ourselves on the
col to feel the full blast, and then struggled back to shelter.

It remained to take the final decision on the morning of the
25th. We were evidently too weak a party to play a waiting game at
this altitude. We must either take our camp to the col or go back. A
serious objection to going forward lay in the shortage of coolies'
rations. Had the men been fit, it would not have been too much for
them to go back to Lhakpa La unladen and reach the north col the
same day. I doubted whether any two could be found to do that
now; and to subtract two was to leave only eight, of whom two were
unfit to go on, so that six would remain to carry seven loads.

However, the distance to the col was so short that I was confident such difficulties could be overcome one way or another. A more unpleasant consideration was the thought of requiring a party which already felt the height too much to sleep at least 1000 feet higher. We might well find it more than we could do to get back over Lhakpa La and be forced to make a hungry descent down the Rongbuk Valley. But there would be no disaster in that event. The crucial matter was the condition of the climbers. It seemed we had not sufficient strength to allow a margin for the unforeseen. And what more were we likely to accomplish from a camp on the north col? The second night had been no less windy than the first. Ever since the weather had cleared the wind had been strong from north-west, and every day we had seen the powdery cloud blown from the mountain crests. The only signs of a change now pointed to no improvement, but rather a fall of snow, by no means an improbable event according to local lore. The arguments, in fact, were all on one side; it would be bad heroics to take wrong risks; and fairly facing the situation one could only admit the necessity of retreat.

It may be added that the real weakness of the party became only too apparent in the course of our return journey over Lhakpa La on this final day; and it must be safe to say that none of the three climbers has ever felt a spasm of regret about the decision to go back or a moment's doubt as to its rightness. It was imposed upon us by circumstances without a reasonable alternative.

No considerations can be more important for future guidance than those affecting the health of the party. But here knowledge will not best be sought from one man's report, even the doctor's. If every member of the expedition were to write a full and frank report of his own health from first to last, with particular reference to the effects of elevation, we might begin to know something about it. I know chiefly in a negative way, and in any case not minutely, how I felt in differing circumstances at various elevations; I know just a little how Bullock was affected, and still less about the coolies. It may possibly be worth adding a few inferences to what has previously been recorded by other parties in the Himalayas.

It is unfortunate for the present purpose that I enjoyed an almost uniform good health at all elevations from first to last. So far as mere living at high altitudes is concerned I observed almost no effects in my own case. My appetite was never-failing. I ate large quantities of solid food, mutton, potatoes, Quaker Oats, bread, and biscuits—whatever presented itself—and it was often decidedly unattractive; and after a day's climbing I had the same craving for sweet things which I have often noticed in the Alps, where, at a place like Zermatt, the consumption of a great number of sweet cakes seems only to stimulate my energy. And I almost invariably slept well at almost all our camps, more lightly perhaps at the higher ones, but with sufficiently refreshing unconsciousness. Comfortable ground, sufficient warmth, a pillow rightly adjusted, all the conditions of a contented body, mattered far more to me than the quality of the air I breathed. On one occasion, after sleeping less well than usual at 17,000 feet, I went up to 20,000 feet and slept in divine oblivion, waking only to see the dawn with fresh delight. Not every one was quite so fortunate as myself. Bullock's appetite, though it improved later to admiration, was notably deficient during the first three weeks for one who was working his body so hard; and he was short of sleep at our highest camps. But in general he seemed hardly to suffer from the fact of living for a few days together at elevations above 17,000 and 18,000 feet. Some other members of the expedition seemed not to be quite at their best at 20,000 feet, and at Lhakpa La were imperfectly refreshed by the night's rest. As to the coolies, I fear their discomforts were apt to increase at the higher camps more than ours, and consequently they may have suffered some loss of sleep, but I have not the slightest evidence to show that after spending a night or several nights at a high camp, except at the last two, they were in any way less fit to go on next day as a consequence of the altitude.[5] It should, perhaps, be added that it seemed in some physical way a relief to come down after staying a long time about 17,000 feet or higher; but on the two occasions when we rested for some days at about 12,000 feet (Kharta), it seemed to me that we were less rather than more fit when we went up again.

Another aspect of this inquiry is the effects of altitude over a longer period. What were the general effects upon health after two or three months? When the party gathered at Kharta, towards the end of August, I observed that most of us seemed remarkably fit; but not so Bullock; he was too thin and appeared to require rest. I dare say he took it with advantage. About myself it is worth remarking that I had completely recovered, with the aid of a tonic, from a nasty visitation of fever and sore throat without coming down to lower altitudes. The last few days of our reconnaissance were a strenuous time, but for the expedition, which, far more than any other, demanded endurance, when we first reached Lhakpa La, I was perfectly fit. Nevertheless, when we went up again on 30 August I was mountain-sick, and never afterwards in September regained my earlier strength. Nor I think did Bullock. It is difficult to account for this deterioration, unless we suppose that altitude, though it may have no immediate effect, takes its toll at length. Wheeler, whose experiences of high camps may be compared with ours, may not agree with this conclusion as fitting his own case; but then his case was different.

Exertion at great heights is another matter, and less dubious in its results. I suppose them to be sufficiently well known. I observed especially: (1) Rapid acclimatisation much as in the Alps, but even more remarkable. (2) Very little relief in coming down; descent was very definitely an exertion, and fatigue continued to increase, especially on gentle slopes; it was necessary to breathe with conscious effort even when descending. (3) The difference between what we could do, say, at 18,000 feet and 20,000 feet was greater in the case of the coolies, whenever they carried loads, than in others. The coolies always appeared to feel the height more quickly. I put this down partly to the fact that few of them really learned either how to breathe or how to husband their strength. Certainly they were much better towards the end, walking rhythmically, but to the last the majority were inclined to hurry. In any case, a small load makes a big difference, but can be compensated largely by reducing pace. (4) Headache was at least as common after descent as before; but personally, so long as I was perfectly fit, and remembered to breathe properly, I did not suffer from headache. (5) A stomach disordered, even in the smallest degree, enormously decreased one's power of endurance. (6) In the last stages, whether as a result of higher altitudes or unfitness I cannot say, a prolonged exertion required more rest—two whole days. This applies to the coolies as well as to myself and others, too, I believe. (7) I was much surprised to find how easily steps might be cut at 21,000 feet. I found myself quite untired after an hour's work in hard ice. (8) We had little experience of rock climbing; but from such as we had (e.g. some steep pitches on one of the peaks which we climbed west of the Rongbuk), I am inclined to think that easy rocks, where one is constantly helping oneself up with arms as well as legs, offer the least tiring way of ascent; and that even comparatively difficult rocks might very well be climbed by fit men up to 23,000 feet.

Finally, it may perhaps be worthy of remark that on the very few occasions when my mind was exerted, I found mental exertion to be tiring at high altitudes and tending to sleeplessness. The life of the lotus-eater was best between expeditions—with perhaps a little piquet.

Is it humanly possible to reach the summit of Everest? We have not a single convincing argument to solve that problem. I felt somehow, when we reached the north col, that the task was not impossible; but that may only have been a delusion based on the appearance of the mountain from that point; it looks much smaller than it is. However, one factor, easily forgotten, is in favour of the assault. The higher one goes the less will be the effect of any given rise. To ascend the 3000 feet above 17,000 is notably less laborious than to ascend the next 3000 up to 23,000 feet; but the atmospheric pressure diminishes less rapidly as one goes up; consequently the difference in effort required between one stage and another should be less at each succeeding stage, and least of all between the last stage and the last but one. I believe it to be possible, at all events, for unladen mountaineers to reach 26,000 feet, and if they can go up so far without exhaustion, I fancy the last 3000 feet will not prove so very much more tiring as to exclude the possibility of their reaching the summit.

But in asserting this bare possibility, which, besides, leaves the coolies out of account, I am very far from a sanguine estimate as to the prospects of success. Before we parted, I put this question to Bullock: 'What are the chances that a given party will get up in a given year?' After considered reflection, he replied: 'Fifty to one against.' That answer also expressed my own feelings. Perhaps at a greater distance from the mountain I am now more sanguine. If men could be found to besiege Everest year after year, I believe it would surrender at last. But the chances against any particular expedition are indeed very large. I assume that principles time-honoured in the Alpine Club will be honoured no less on Mount Everest than on other mountains. Climbers, of course, are always taking risks; but there are some which experience and *a priori* reason alike reject. A party of two arriving at the top, each so tired that he is beyond helping the other, might provide good copy for the press, but the performance would provoke the censure of reasonable opinion. If any one falls sick at the last camp, he must be taken down with an adequate escort and as soon as possible; and similarly on the final day. And coolies who become exhausted in carrying up their loads cannot be allowed to make their own way down; exhausted they are incompetent, and must be properly looked after. It is with such difficulties and such necessities that we have to reckon; and any reckoning, I believe, which fairly weighs the conditions and circumstances governing such an enterprise can only come to the conclusion that the chances in favour of success for any particular party are small indeed.

* * *

Read at the Joint Meeting of the Royal Geographical Society and the Alpine Club on 20 December 1921, Published as 'Mount Everest: The Reconnaissance' *Alpine Journal*, Vol. 34 p 215ff.

6

BLACK CLIFFS

The Reconnaissance of Mount Everest, 1921

As a matter of history, the highest mountain in the world attracted attention so early as 1850. When we started our travels in 1921, something was already known about it from a surveyor's point of view; it was a triangulated peak with a position on the map; but from the mountaineer's point of view almost nothing was known. Mount Everest had been seen and photographed from various points on the Singalila ridge as well as from Khampa Dzong; from these photographs it may dimly be made out that snow lies on the upper part of the Eastern face at no very steep angle, while the arête bounding this face on the North comes down gently for a considerable distance. But the whole angle subtended at the great summit by the distance between the two of these view-points which are farthest apart is only 54°. The North-west sides of the mountain had never been photographed and nothing was known of its lower parts anywhere. Perhaps the distant view most valuable to a mountaineer is that from Sandakphu, because it suggests gigantic precipices on the South side of the mountain so that he need have no regrets that access is barred in that direction for political reasons.

The present reconnaissance began at Khampa Dzong, no less than two miles away, and in consequence of misfortunes which the reader will not have forgotten was necessarily entrusted to Mr G.H. Bullock and myself, the only representatives of the Alpine Club now remaining in the Expedition. It may seem an irony of fate that actually on the day after the distressing event of Dr. Kellas's death we experienced the strange elation of seeing Everest for the first time. It was a perfect early morning as we plodded up the barren slopes above our camp, rising behind the old rugged fort which is itself a singularly impressive and dramatic spectacle; we had mounted perhaps a thousand feet when we stayed and turned, and saw what we came to see. There was no mistaking the two great peaks in the West: that to the left must be Makalu, grey, severe and yet distinctly graceful, and the other away to the right—who could doubt its identity? It was a prodigious white fang excrescent from the jaw of the world. We saw Mount Everest not quite sharply defined on account of a slight haze in that direction; this circumstance added a touch of mystery and grandeur; we were satisfied that the highest of mountains would not disappoint us. And we learned one fact of great importance: the lower parts of the mountain were hidden by the range of nearer mountains clearly shown in the map running North from the Nila La and now called the Gyangkar Range, but it was possible to distinguish all that showed near Everest beyond them by a difference in tone, and we were certain that one great rocky peak appearing a little way to the left of Everest must belong to its near vicinity.

It was inevitable, as we proceeded to the West from Khamba Dzong, that we should lose sight of Mount Everest; after a few miles even its tip was obscured by the Gyangkar Range, and we naturally began to wonder whether it would not be possible to ascend one of these nearer peaks which must surely give us a wonderful view. I had hopes that we should be crossing the range by a high pass, in which case it would be a simple matter to ascend some eminence near it. But at Tinki we learned that our route would lie in the gorge to the North of the mountains where the river Yaru cuts its way through from the East to join the Arun.

From Gyangkar Nangpa, which lies under a rocky summit over 20,000 feet high, Bullock and I, on 11 June, made an early start and proceeded down the gorge. It was a perfect morning and for once we had tolerably swift animals to ride; we were fortunate in choosing the right place to ford the river and our spirits were high. How could they be otherwise? Ever since we had lost sight of Everest the Gyangkar Mountains had been our ultimate horizon to the West. Day by day as we had approached them our thoughts had concentrated more and more upon what lay beyond. On the far side was a new country. Now the great Arun River was to divulge its secrets and we should see Everest again after nearly halving the distance. The nature of the gorge was such that our curiosity could not be satisfied until the last moment. After crossing the stream we followed the flat margin of its right bank until the cliffs converging to the exit were towering above us. Then in a minute we were out on the edge of a wide sandy basin stretching away with complex undulations to further hills. Sand and barren hills as before—but with a difference; for we saw the long Arun Valley proceeding Southwards to cut through the Himalayas and its western arm which we should have to follow to Tingri; and there were marks of more ancient river beds and strange inland lakes. It was a desolate scene, I suppose; no flowers were to be seen nor any sign of life beyond some stunted gorse bushes on a near hillside and a few patches of coarse brown grass, and the only habitations were dry inhuman ruins; but whatever else was dead, our interest was alive.

After a brief halt a little way out in the plain, to take our bearings and speculate where the great mountains should appear, we made our way up a steep hill to a rocky crest overlooking the gorge. The only visible snow mountains were in Sikkim. Kanchenjunga was clear and eminent; we had never seen it so fine before; it now seemed singularly strong and monumental, like the leonine face of some splendid musician with a glory of white hair. In the direction of Everest no snow mountain appeared. We saw the long base tongues descending into the Arun Valley from the Gyangkar Range, above them in the middle distance an amazingly sharp rock summit and below a blue depth most unlike Tibet as we had known it hitherto. A conical hill stood sentinel at the far end of the valley, and in the distance was a bank of clouds.

Our attention was engaged by the remarkable spike of rock, a proper aiguille. As we were observing it a rift opened in the clouds behind; at first we had merely a fleeting glimpse of some mountain evidently much more distant, then a larger and clearer view revealed a recognisable form; it was Makalu appearing just where it should be according to our calculations with map and compass.

We were now able to make out almost exactly where Everest should be; but the clouds were dark in that direction. We gazed at them intently through field glasses as though by some miracle we might pierce the veil. Presently the miracle happened. We caught the gleam of snow behind the grey mists. A whole group of mountains began to appear in gigantic fragments. Mountain shapes are often fantastic seen through a mist; these were like the wildest creation of a dream. A preposterous triangular lump rose out of the depths; its edge came leaping up at an angle of about 70° and ended nowhere. To the left a black serrated crest was hanging in the sky incredibly. Gradually, very gradually, we saw the great mountain sides and glaciers and arêtes, now one fragment and now another through the floating rifts, until far higher in the sky than imagination had dared to suggest the white summit of Everest appeared. And in this series of partial glimpses we had seen a whole; we were able to piece together the fragments, to interpret the dream. However much might remain to be understood, the centre had a clear meaning as one mountain shape, the shape of Everest.

It is hardly possible of course from a distance of 57 miles to formulate an accurate idea of a mountain's shape. But some of its most remarkable features may be distinguished for what they are. We were looking at Everest from about North-east and evidently a long arête was thrust out towards us. Some little distance below the summit the arête came down to a black shoulder, which we conjectured would be an insuperable obstacle. To the right of this we saw the skyline in profile and judged it not impossibly steep. The edge was probably a true arête because it appeared to be joined by a col to a sharp peak to the North. From the direction of this col a valley came down to the East and evidently drained into the Arun. This was one fact of supreme importance which was now established and we noticed that it agreed with what was shown on the map; the map in fact went up in our esteem and we were inclined hereafter to believe in its veracity until we established the contrary. Another fact was even more remarkable. We knew something more about the great peak near Everest which we had seen from Khamba Dzong; we knew now that it was not a separate mountain; in a sense it was part of Everest, or rather Everest was not one mountain but two; this great black mountain to the South was connected with Everest by a continuous arête and divided from it only by a snow col which must itself be at least 27,000 feet high. The black cliffs of this mountain, which faced us, were continuous with the icy East face of Everest itself.

A bank of cloud still lay across the face of the mountain when Bullock and I left the crest where we were established. It was late in the afternoon. We had looked down into the gorge and watched our little donkeys crossing the stream. Now we proceeded to follow their tracks across the plain. The wind was fiercely blowing up the sand and swept it away to leeward, transforming the dead flat surface into a wriggling sea of watered silk. The party were all sheltering in their tents when we rejoined them. Our camp was situated on a grassy bank below which by some miracle a spring wells out from the sand. We also sought shelter. But a short while after sunset the wind subsided. We all came forth and proceeded to a little eminence near at hand; and as we looked down the valley there was Everest calm in the stillness of evening and clear in the last light.

I have dwelt upon this episode at some length partly because in our travels before we reached the mountain it is for me beyond her adventures, and unforgettable; and not less because the vision of Everest inhabiting our minds after this day had no small influence upon our deductions when we came to close quarters with the mountain. We made other opportunities before reaching Tingri to ascend likely hills for what we could see; notably from Shekar Dzong we made a divergence from the line of march and from a hill above Ponglet, on a morning of cloudless sunrise, saw the whole group of mountains of which Everest is the centre. But no view was so instructive as that above Shiling and we added little to the knowledge gained that day.

On 23 June, after a day's interval to arrange stores, the climbing party set forth from Tingri Dzong. We were two Sahibs, sixteen coolies, a Sirdar, Gyalzen and a cook, Dukpa. The process of selecting the coolies had been begun some time before this; the long task of nailing their boots had been nearly completed on the march and we were now confident that sixteen of the best Sherpa with their climbing boots, ice axes and each a suit of underwear would serve us well. The Sirdar through whom coolies had been engaged in the first instance seemed to understand what we wanted and to have sufficient authority, and Dukpa, though we could not expect from him any culinary refinements, had shown himself a person of some energy and competence who should do much to reduce the discomforts of life in camp. Our equipment was seriously deficient in one respect: we were short of words. A few hours spent in Darjeeling with a *Grammar of Tibetan* had easily convinced me that I should profit little in the short time available by the study of that language. It had been assumed by both Bullock and myself that our experienced leaders would give the necessary orders for organisation in any dialect that might be required. We had found little opportunity since losing them to learn a language, and our one hope of conversing with the Sirdar was a vocabulary of about 150 words which I had written down in a notebook to be committed to memory on the march and consulted when occasion should arise.

The task before us was not likely to prove a simple and straight forward matter, and we had no expectation that it would be quickly concluded. It would be necessary in the first place to find the mountain; as we looked across the wide plains from Tingri and saw the dark monsoon clouds gathered in all directions we were not reassured. And there would be more than one approach to be found. We should have to explore a number of valleys radiating from Everest and separated by high ridges which would make lateral communication extremely difficult; we must learn from which direction various parts of the mountain could most conveniently be reached. And beyond all investigation of the approaches we should have to scrutinise Mount Everest itself. Our reconnaissance must aim at a complete knowledge of the various faces and arêtes, a correct understanding of the whole form and structure of the mountain and the distribution of its various parts; we must distinguish the vulnerable places in its armour and finally pit our skill against the obstacles wherever an opportunity of ascent should appear until all such opportunities were exhausted. The whole magnitude of the enterprise was very present in our minds as we left Tingri. We decided that a preliminary reconnaissance should include the first two aims of finding the approaches to Mount Everest and determining its shape, while anything in the nature of an assault should be left to the last as a separate stage of organisation and effort. In the result we may claim to have kept these ends in view without allowing the less important to prey upon the greater. So long as a doubt remained as to the way we should choose we made no attempt to climb the peak; we required ourselves first to find out as much as possible by more distant observations.

Mount Everest, as it turned out, did not prove difficult to find. Almost in the direct line from Tingri are two great peaks respectively 26,870 and 25,990 feet high—known to the Survey of India as M1 and M2 and to Tibetans as Cho-Uyo and Gyachung Kang. They lie about W.N.W. of Everest. We had to decide whether we should pass to the South of them, leaving them on our left, or to the North. In the first case we surmised that we might find ourselves to the South of a Western arête of Everest, and possibly in Nepal, which was out of bounds. The arête, if it existed, might perhaps be reached from the North and give us the view we should require of the South-western side, in which case one base would serve us for a large area of investigation and we should economise time that would otherwise be spent in moving our camp round from one side to another. Consequently we chose the Northern approach. We learned from local knowledge that in two days we might reach a village and monastery called Chöbu, and from there could follow a long valley to Everest. And so it proved. Chöbu was not reached without some difficulty, but this was occasioned not by obstacles in the country but by the manners of Tibetans. At Tingri we had hired four pack animals. We had proceeded two or three miles across the plain when we perceived they were heading in the wrong direction. We were trusting to the guidance of their local drivers and felt very uncertain as to where exactly we should be aiming; but their line was about 60° to the South of our objective according to a guesswork compass bearing. An almost interminable three-cornered argument followed. It appeared that our guides intended to take five days to Chöbu. They knew all about 'ca canny'. In the end we decided to take the risk of a separation; Gyalzen went with the bullocks and our tents to change transport at the village where we were intended to stay the night, while the rest of us made a bee-line for a bridge where we should have to cross the Rongbuk stream. At the foot of a vast moraine we waited on the edge of the 'maidan', anxiously hoping that we should see some sign of fresh animals approaching; and at length we saw them. It was a late camp that evening on a strip of meadow beside the stream, but we had the comfort of reflecting that we had foiled the natives, whose aim was to retard our progress; and in the sequel we reached our destination with no further trouble.

Cho-Uyo

On 25 June we crossed the stream at Chöbu. Tibetan bridges are so constructed as to offer the passenger ample opportunities of experiencing the sensation of insecurity and contemplating the possibilities of disaster. This one was no exception. We had no wish to risk our stores, and it was planned that the beasts should swim. They were accordingly unladen and driven with yell and blow by a willing crowd, until one more frightened than the rest plunged into the torrent and the others followed. We now found ourselves on the right bank of the Rongbuk stream, and knew we had but to follow it up to reach the glacier at the head of the valley. An hour or so above Chöbu we entered a gorge with high red cliffs above us on the left. Below them was a little space of fertile ground where the moisture draining down from the limestone above was caught before it reached the stream—a green ribbon stretched along the margin with grass and low bushes, yellow-flowering asters, rhododendrons and juniper. I think we had never seen anything so green since we came up on to the tableland of Tibet. It was a day of brilliant sunshine, as yet warm and windless. The memory of Alpine meadows came into my mind. I remembered their manifold allurements; I could almost smell the scent of pines. Now I was filled with the desire to lie here in this 'oasis' and live at ease and sniff the clean fragrance of mountain plants. But we went on, on and up the long valley winding across a broad stony bay; and all the stony hillsides under the midday sun were alike monotonously dreary. At length we followed the path up a steeper rise crowned by two chortens between which it passes. We paused here in sheer astonishment. Perhaps we had half expected to see Mount Everest at this moment. In the back of my mind were a host of questions about it clamouring for answer. But the sight of it now banished every thought. We forgot the stony wastes and regrets for other beauties. We asked no questions and made no comment, but simply looked.

It is perhaps because Everest presented itself so dramatically on this occasion that I find the Northern aspect more particularly imaged in my mind, when I recall the mountain. But in any case this aspect has a special significance. The Rongbuk Valley is well constructed to show off the peak at its head; for about 20 miles it is extraordinarily straight and in that distance rises only 4,000 feet, the glacier, which is 10 miles long, no more steeply than the rest. In consequence of this arrangement one has only to be raised very slightly above the bed of the valley to see it almost as a flat way up to the very head of the glacier from which the cliffs of Everest spring. To the place where Everest stands one looks along rather than up. The glacier is prostrate; not a part of the mountain; not even a pediment; merely a floor footing the high walls. At the end of the valley and above the glacier Everest rises not so much a peak as a prodigious mountain-mass. There is no complication for the eye. The highest of the world's great mountains, it seems, has to make but a single gesture of magnificence to be lord of all, vast in unchallenged and isolated supremacy. To the discerning eye other mountains are visible, giants between 23,000 and 26,000 feet high. Not one of their slenderer heads even reaches their chief's shoulder; beside Everest they escape notice—such is the pre-eminence of the greatest.

Considered as a structure Mount Everest is seen from the Rongbuk Valley to achieve height with amazing simplicity. The steep wall 10,000 feet high is contained between two colossal members—to the left the North-eastern arête, which leaves the summit at a gentle angle and in a distance of about half a mile descends only 1,000 feet before turning more sharply downwards from a clearly defined shoulder; and to the right the North-west arête (its true direction is about W.N.W.), which comes down steeply from the summit but makes up for the weaker nature of this support by immense length below. Such is the broad plan. In one respect it is modified. The wide angle between the two main arêtes involves perhaps too long a face; a further support is added. The Northern face is brought out a little below the North-east shoulder and then turned back to meet the crest again, so that from the point of the shoulder a broad arête leads down to the North and is connected by a snow col at about 23,000 feet with a Northern wing of mountains which forms the right bank of the Rongbuk Glacier and to some extent masks the view of the lower parts of Everest. Nothing could be stronger than this arrangement and it is nowhere fantastic. We do not see jagged crests and a multitude of pinnacles, and beautiful as such ornament may be we do not miss it. The outline is comparatively smooth because the stratification is horizontal, a circumstance which seems again to give strength, emphasising the broad foundations. And yet Everest is a rugged giant. It has not the smooth undulations of a snow mountain with white cap and glaciated flanks. It is rather a great rock mass, coated often with a thin layer of white powder which is blown about its sides, and bearing perennial snow only on the gentler ledges and on several wide faces less steep than the rest. One such place is the long arm of the North-west arête which with its slightly articulated buttresses is like the nave of a vast cathedral roofed with snow. I was, in fact, reminded often by this Northern view of Winchester Cathedral with its long high nave and low square tower; it is only at a considerable distance that one appreciates the great height of this building and the strength which seems capable of supporting a far taller tower. Similarly with Everest; the summit lies back so far along the immense arêtes that big as it always appears one required a distant view to realise its height; and it has no spire though it might easily bear one; I have thought sometimes that a Matterhorn might be piled on the top of Everest and the gigantic structure would support the added weight in stable equanimity.

On 26 June we pitched our tents in full view of Everest and a little way beyond the large monastery of Chöyling which provides the habitations nearest to the mountain, about 16 miles away. After three days' march from the Expedition's headquarters at Tingri we had found the object of our quest and established a base in the Rongbuk Valley, which was to serve us for a month.

The first steps in a prolonged reconnaissance such as we were proposing to undertake were easily determined by topographical circumstances. Neither Bullock nor I was previously acquainted with any big mountains outside the Alps; to our experience in the Alps we had continually to refer, both for understanding this country and for estimating the efforts required to reach a given point in it. The Alps provided a standard of comparison which alone could be our guide until we had acquired some fresh knowledge in the new surroundings. No feature of what we saw so immediately challenged this comparison as the glacier ahead of us; in so narrow a glacier it was hardly surprising that the lower part of it should be covered with stones, but higher the whole surface was white ice, and the white ice came down in a broad stream tapering gradually to a point when it was lost in the waste of the brown grey. What was the meaning of this? Even from a distance it was possible to make out that the white stream contained pinnacles of ice. Was it all composed of pinnacles? Would they prove an insuperable obstacle? In the Alps the main glaciers are most usually highways, the ways offered to the climber for his travelling. Were they not to prove highways here?

Our first expedition was designed to satisfy our curiosity on this head. Allowing a bountiful margin of time for untoward contingencies we set forth on 27 June with five coolies at 3.15 a.m., and made our way up the valley with a good moon to help us. To be tramping under the stars toward a great mountain is always an adventure; now we were adventuring for the first time in a new mountain country which still held in store for us all its surprises and almost all its beauties. It was not our plan at present to make any allowance for the special condition of elevation; we expected to learn how that condition would tell and how to make allowances for the future. We started from our camp at 6,000 feet—above the summit of Mont Blanc—just as we should have left an Alpine hut 6,000 feet lower, and when we took our first serious halt at 7 a.m. had already crossed the narrow end of the glacier. That short experience—an hour or so—was sufficient for the moment. The hummocks of ice covered with stones of all sizes—like the huge waves of a brown angry sea—gave us no chance of ascending the glacier; one might hopefully follow a trough for a little distance but invariably to be stopped by the necessity of mounting once more to a crest and descending again on the other side. Nevertheless, we were not dissatisfied with our progress. We were now in a stream bed between the glacier and its left bank and above the exit of the main glacier stream, which comes out on this side well above the snout. The watercourse offered an opportunity of progress; it was dry almost everywhere and for a bout of leaping from boulder to boulder we were usually rewarded by a space of milder walking on the flat sandy bed. Our pace I considered entirely satisfactory as we went on after breakfast; unconsciously I was led into something like a race by one of the coolies who was pressing along at my side. I noticed that though he was slightly built he seemed extremely strong and active, compact of muscle; but he had not yet learnt the art of walking rhythmically and balancing easily from stone to stone. I wondered how long he would keep up. Presently we came to a corner where our stream bed ended and a small glacier-snout was visible above us, apparently descending from the North-west. We gathered on a high bank of stones to look out over the glacier. I observed now that the whole aspect of the party had changed. The majority were more than momentarily tired; they were visibly suffering from some sort of malaise. It was not yet nine o'clock and we had risen barely 2,000 feet, but their spirits had gone. There were grunts instead of laughter.

The glacier's left bank which we were following was now trending to the right. To the South and standing in front of the great North-west arm of Everest was a comparatively small and very attractive snow peak, perhaps a little less than 21,000 feet high. We had harboured a vague ambition to reach its shoulder, a likely point for prospecting the head of the Rongbuk Glacier. But between us and this objective was a wide stretch of hummocky ice which had every appearance of being something more than a mere bay of the main glacier. We suspected a Western branch and proceeded to confirm our suspicion. After a rough crossing below the glacier above us we were fortunate enough to find another trough wider than the first and having a flat sandy bottom where we walked easily enough. Presently leaving the coolies to rest on the edge of the glacier Bullock and I mounted a high stony shoulder, and from there, at 18,500 feet, saw the glacier stretching away to the West, turning sharply below us to rise more steeply than before. Cloud prevented us from distinguishing what appeared to be a high mountain ridge at the far end of it.

It was evident that nothing was to be gained at present by pushing our investigations further to the West. Our curiosity was as yet unsatisfied about those white spires of ice to which our eyes had constantly returned. We declined the alternative of retracing our steps and without further delay set about to cross the glacier. It was now eleven o'clock and we were under no delusion that the task before us would be other than arduous and long. But the reward in interest and valuable information promised to be great, for, by exploring the glacier's right bank during our descent, we should learn all we wanted to know before making plans for an advance. And we hoped to be in before dark.

The stone-covered ice on which we first embarked compared favourably with that of our earlier experience before breakfast. The sea, so to speak, was not so choppy; the waves were longer. We were able to follow convenient troughs for considerable distances. But at the bottom of a trough which points whither it will it is impossible to keep a definite direction and difficult to know to what extent one is erring. An hour's hard work was required to bring us to the edge of the white ice. Our first question was answered at a glance. It had always seemed improbable that these were séracs such as one meets on an Alpine icefall, and clearly they were not. We saw no signs of lateral crevasses. The shapes were comparatively conical and regular, not delicately poised but firmly based, safely perpendicular and not dangerously impending. They were the result not of movement but of melting, and it was remarkable that on either side the black ice looked over the white, as though the glacier had sunk in the middle. The pinnacles resembled a topsy-turvy system of colossal icicles, icicles thrust upwards from a common icy mass, the whole resting on a definable floor. The largest were about 50 feet high.

We were divided from this fairy world of spires by a deep boundary moat and entered it on the far side by what may be described as a door but that it had no lintel. An alley led us over a low wall and we had reached the interior. A connected narrative of our wanderings in this amazing country could hardly be true to its disconnected character. The White Rabbit himself would have been bewildered here. No course seemed to lead anywhere. Our idea was to keep to the floor so far as we were able; but most usually we were scrambling up a chimney or slithering down one, cutting round the foot of a tower or actually traversing along an icy crest. To be repeatedly crossing little cols with the continued expectation of seeing a way beyond was a sufficiently exciting labour; it was also sufficiently laborious since the chopping of steps was necessary almost everywhere; but fatigue was out of sight in the enchanted scene, with the cool delight of little lakes, of the ice reflected in their unruffled waters and of blue sky showing between the white spires. We had but one misadventure, and that of no consequence—it was my fate when crossing the frozen surface of one little lake to suffer a sudden immersion: the loss of dignity perhaps was more serious than the chilling of ardour, for we soon came upon a broadening alley and came out from our labyrinth as suddenly as we entered it, to lie and bask in the warm sun.

Our crossing of the white ice after all had taken little more than two hours, and we might well consider ourselves fortunate. But it must be remembered that we were far from fresh at the start and now the reaction set in. The stone-covered glacier on this side, besides being a much narrower belt, was clearly not going to give us trouble, and after an ample halt we started across it easily enough. On the right bank we had noticed many hours before above the glacier a broad flat shelf, presumably an old moraine, and a clear mark along the hillside away down to a point below the snout. This was now our objective and no doubt once we had gained it our troubles would be ended. But in the first place it had to be gained. In the Alps it has often seemed laborious to go up hill towards the end of a day: it was a new sensation to find it an almost impossible exertion to drag oneself up a matter of 150 feet. And further exertions were to be required of us. A little way down the valley a glacier stream came in on our right; we had observed this before and hopefully expected to follow our terrace round and rejoin it on the far side of the gully. But it was late in the afternoon and the stream was at its fullest. We followed it down with defeated expectations; it always proved just too dangerous to cross. Finally it formed a lake at the edge of the glacier before disappearing beneath it and obliged us to make a detour on the ice once more. I suppose this obstacle was mild enough; but again an ascent was involved, and after it at least one member of the party seemed incapable of further effort. Another halt was necessary. We were now down to about 17,000 feet and at the head of a long passage at the side of the glacier, similar to that we had ascended in the morning on the other bank. Those who suffer from altitude on a mountain have a right to expect a recovery on the descent. But I saw no signs of one yet. It was a long painful hour balancing from boulder to boulder along the passage, with the conscious effort of keeping up the feat until we came out into the flat basin at the glacier end. Then as we left the glacier behind us the day seemed to come right. One obstacle remained, a stream which had been crossed with difficulty in the morning and was now swollen to a formidable torrent. It was carried with a rush—this was no moment for delay. Each man chose his own way for a wetting; for my part, after a series of exciting leaps on to submerged stones I landed in the deepest part of the stream with the pick of my axe dug into the far bank to help me scramble out. After this I remember only of the last four miles the keen race against the gathering darkness; fatigue was forgotten and we reached camp at 8.15 p.m., tired perhaps, but not exhausted.

It has seemed necessary to given an account of this first expedition in some detail in order to emphasise certain conditions which governed all our movements from the Rongbuk Valley. We now knew how to get about. Flat though the glacier might be, it was no use for travelling in any part we had seen, not a road but an obstacle. The obstacle, however, had not proved unsurmountable, and though the crossing had been laborious and long, we were not convinced that it need be so long another time; careful reconnaissance might reveal a better way, and we had little doubt that both the main glacier and its Western branch could be used freely for lateral communication if we chose. It would not always be necessary in organising an expedition to be encamped on one side of the glacier rather than the other. And we had discovered that it was not a difficult matter to make our way along the glacier sides; we could choose either a trough or a shelf.

We had also been greatly interested by the phenomena of fatigue. The most surprising fact when we applied our standard of comparison was that coming down had proved so laborious; Bullock and I had each discovered independently that we got along better when we remembered to breathe hard, and we already suspected what we afterwards established that it was necessary to adopt a conscious method of breathing deeply for coming down as for going up. Another inference, subsequently confirmed on many occasions, accused the glacier. The mid-day sun had been hot as we crossed it and I seemed to notice some enervating influence which had not affected me elsewhere. It was the glacier that had knocked me out, not the hard work alone but some malignant quality in the atmosphere, which I can neither describe nor explain; and in crossing a glacier during the day I always afterwards observed the same effect; I might feel as fit and fresh as I could wish on the moraine at the side but only once succeeded in crossing a glacier without feeling a despairing lassitude.

I shall now proceed to quote from my diary:

28 June A slack day in camp. It is difficult to induce coolies to take any steps to make themselves more comfortable. We're lucky to have this fine weather. The mountain appears not to be intended for climbing. I've no inclination to think about it in steps to the summit. Nevertheless, we gaze much through field-glasses. E. is, generally speaking, convex, steep in lower parts and slanting back to summit. Last section of East arête[6] should go; but rocks up to the shoulder are uninviting. An arête must join up here, coming down towards us and connecting up with first peak to N [the North Peak (Changtse)]. There's no true North arête to the summit, as we had supposed at first. It's more like this:

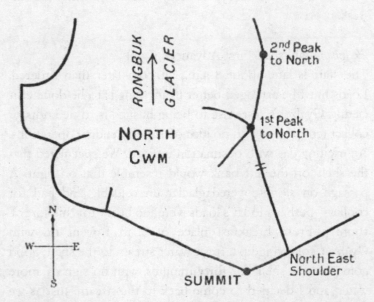

G.H.B. thinks little of the North-west arm. But I'm not so sure; much easier going on that snow if we can get to it and rocks above probably easier than they look—steep but broken. Are we seeing the true edge? I wish some folk at home could see the precipice on this side—a grim spectacle most unlike the long gentle snow slopes suggested by photos. Amusing to think how one's vision of the last effort has changed; it looked like crawling half-blind up easy snow, an even slope all the way up from a camp on a flat snow shoulder; but it won't be that sort of grind; we'll want climbers and not half-dazed ones; a tougher job than I bargained for, sanguine as usual.

E. is a rock mountain.

Obviously we must get round to the West first. The Western glacier looks as flat as this one. Perhaps we shall be able to walk round into another cwm [*cwm, combe or corry*—the rounded head of a valley] on the far side of North-west buttress.

29 June Established First Advanced Camp.

The start is late, about 8 a.m., an hour later than ordered. Loads must be arranged better if anything is to be done efficiently. Gyalzen's response to being hustled is to tie knots or collect tent pegs—with no idea of superintending operations. An exciting day with destination unfixed. We speculated that the shelf on the left bank would resemble that on right. A passage on stone-covered glacier unavoidable and bad for coolies—perhaps today's loads were too heavy for this sort of country. From breakfast place of 27th I went on with Gyalzen, following up a fresh-water stream to the shelf; good going on this shelf for forty minutes, with no sign of more water, and I decided to come back to the stream. Just as we were turning I saw a pond of water and a spring, an ideal place, and it's much better to be further on. Real good luck. Wind blows down the glacier and the camp is well sheltered. Only crab that we lose the sun early—4 p.m. today; but on the other hand it should hit us very soon after sunrise.

Coolies in between 3.30 and 4.30. Dorji Gompa first, stout fellow, with a big load. They seem happy and interested…. It should now be possible to carry reconnaissance well up the main glacier and to the basin Westwards without moving further—once we get accustomed to this elevation.

30 June A short day with second[7] party, following the shelf to a corner which marks roughly the junction of the main glacier with its Western branch. A clearing day after a good night; we found a good way across to the opposite corner, about an hour across, and came back in leisurely fashion. Neither B. nor I felt fit.

6b
Continued...

The reader will gather from these notes some idea of the whole nature of our problem and the subjects of our most anxious thoughts. The camp established on 25 June lasted us until 8 July. Meanwhile the idea was growing, the vision of Everest as a structural whole, and of the glaciers and lower summits to North and West. This idea resembled the beginning of an artist's painting, a mere rough design at the start, but growing by steps of clearer definition in one part and another towards the precise completion of a whole. For us the mountain parts defined themselves in the mind as the result of various expeditions. We set out to gain a point of view with particular questions to be answered; partial answers and a new point of view stimulated more curiosity, other questions, and again the necessity to reach a particular place whence we imagined they might best be answered. And at the same time another aim had to be kept in mind. The coolies, though mountain-men, were not mountaineers. They had to be trained in the craft of mountaineering, in treading safely on snow or ice in dangerous places, in climbing easy rocks and most particularly in the use of rope and ice-axe—and this not merely for our foremost needs, but to ensure that, whenever we were able to launch an assault upon Mount Everest, and all would be put to the most exhausting test, they should have that reserve strength of a practised balance and ordered method on which security must ultimately depend.

On 1 July I set out with five coolies to reach the head of the great cwm under the North face of Mount Everest. The snow on the upper glacier was soft and made very heavy going. Bad weather came up and in a race against the clouds we were beaten and failed to find out what happened to the glacier at its Western head under the North-west arête. My view of the col lying between Everest and the North Peak (Changtse)—the North Col as we now began to call it, or in Tibetan Chang La—was also unsatisfactory; but I saw enough to make out a broken glacier running up Eastwards towards the gap with steep and uninviting snow slopes under the pass. I was now sure that before attempting to reach this col from the Rongbuk Glacier, if ever we determined to reach it, we should have to reconnoitre the other side and if possible find a more hopeful alternative; moreover, from a nearer inspection of the slopes below the Northwest arête I was convinced that they could be chosen for an attack only as a last resort; if anything were to be attempted here, we must find a better way up from the East.

I had vaguely hoped to bring the party home sufficiently fresh to climb again on the following day. But the fatigue of going in deep snow for three hours up the glacier, though we had been no higher than 19,100 feet, had been too great, and again we had noticed only a slight relief in coming down; it was a tired party that dragged back over the glacier crossing and into camp at 6.15 p.m., thirteen hours after starting.

3 July was devoted to an expedition designed chiefly to take coolies on to steeper ground and at the same time to explore the small glacier which we had observed above us on the first day to the North-west; by following up the terrace from our present camp we could now come to the snout of it in half an hour or less. After working up the glacier we made for a snow col between two high peaks. On reaching a bergschrund we found above its upper lip hard ice, which continued no doubt to the ridge. While Bullock looked

after the party below I cut a staircase slanting up to a small island of rock two feet away; from that security I began to bring the party up. We had now the interesting experience of seeing our coolies for the first time on real hard ice; it was not a convincing spectacle, as they made their way up with the ungainly movements of beginners; and though the last man never left the secure anchorage of the bergschrund, the proportion of two Sahibs to five coolies seemed lamentably weak, and when one man slipped from the steep steps at an awkward corner, though Bullock was able to hold him, it was clearly time to retire. But the descent was a better performance; the coolies were apt pupils, and we felt that with practice on the glacier the best of them should become safe mountaineers. And on this day we had reached a height of 21,000 feet[8] from our camp at 17,500 feet. I had the great satisfaction of observing that one could cut steps quite happily at this altitude. The peak lying to the North of the col, which had been our objective on this day, attracted our attention by its position; we thought it should have a commanding view over all this complicated country, and after a day in camp very pleasantly spent in receiving a visit from Colonel Howard-Bury and Dr. Heron, set out on 5 July determined to reach its summit. The start was made at 4.15 a.m. in the first light, an hour earlier than usual; we proceeded up the stone shoots immediately above our camp and after a halt for photography at the glorious moment of sunrise had made 2,500 feet and reached the high shoulder above us at 7 a.m. This place was connected with our peak by a snowy col which had now to be reached by a long traverse over a South-facing slope. Though the angle was not steep very little snow was lying here, and where the ice was peeping through it was occasionally necessary to cut steps. I felt it was a satisfactory performance to reach the col at 9.30 a.m.; the coolies had come well, though one of them was burdened with the quarter-plate camera; but evidently their efforts had already tired them. Ahead of us was a long, curving snow arête, slightly corniced and leading ultimately to a rocky shoulder. We thought that once this shoulder was gained the summit would be within our reach. Shortly after we went on two coolies dropped out, and by 11.30 a.m. the rest had given up the struggle. It was fortunate that they fell out here and not later, for they were able to make their way down in our tracks and regain the col below in safety. The angle steepened as we went on very slowly now, but still steadily enough, until we reached the rocks, a frail slatey structure with short perpendicular pitches. From the shoulder onwards my memories are dim. I have the impression of a summit continually receding from the position imagined by sanguine hopes and of a task growing constantly more severe, of steeper sides, of steps to be cut, of a dwindling pace, more frequent little halts standing where we were, and of breathing quicker but no less deep and always conscious; the respiratory engine had to be kept running as the indispensable source of energy, and ever as we went on more work was required of it. At last we found ourselves without an alternative under an icy wall; but the ice was a delusion; in the soft flaky substance smothering rocks behind it we had strength left to cut a way up to the crest again, and after a few more steps were on the summit itself.

It was now 2.45 p.m. The aneroid used by Bullock, which, after comparison with one of Howard-Bury's was supposed to read low, registered 23,050 feet,[9] and we puffed out our chests as we examined it, computing that we had risen from our camp over 5,500 feet. The views both earlier in the day and at this moment were of the highest interest. To the East we had confirmed our impression of the North Peak as having a high ridge stretching eastwards and forming the side of whatever valley connected with the Arun River in this direction; the upper parts of Everest's North face had been clearly visible for a long time, and we could now be certain that they lay back at no impossibly steep angle, more particularly above the North Col and up to the North-east shoulder. All we had seen immediately to the West of the mountain had been of the greatest interest, and had suggested the idea that the crinkled summit there might be connected not directly with Mount Everest itself, but only by way of the South Peak. And finally we now saw the connections of all that lay around us with the two great triangulated peaks away to the West, Gyachung Kang, 25,990 and Cho-Uyo, 26,870 feet. While complaining of the clouds which had come up as usual during the morning to spoil our view we were not dissatisfied with the expansion of our knowledge and we were elated besides to be where we were. But our situation was far from perfectly secure. The ascent had come very near to exhausting our strength; for my part I felt distinctly mountain-sick; we might reflect that we should not be obliged to cut more steps, but we should have to proceed downwards with perfect accuracy of balance and a long halt was desirable. However, the clouds were now gathering about us, dark thunder-clouds come up from the North and threatening; it was clear we must not wait; after fifteen minutes on the summit we started down at three o'clock. Fortune favoured us. The wind was no more than a breeze; a few flakes of snow were unnoticed in our flight; the temperature was mild; the storm's malice was somehow dissipated with no harm done. We rejoined the coolies before five o'clock and were back in our camp at 7.15 p.m., happy to have avoided a descent in the dark.

Our next plan, based on our experience of this long mountain ridge, was to practise the coolies in the use of crampons on hard snow and ice. But snow fell heavily on the night of the 6th; we deferred our project. It was the beginning of worse weather; the monsoon was breaking in earnest. And though crampons afterwards came up to our camps wherever we went they were not destined to help us, and in the event were never used.

On 8 July we moved up with a fresh party of seven coolies, taking only our lightest tents and no more than was necessary for three nights, in the hope that by two energetic expeditions we should reach the Western cwm which, we suspected, must exist on the far

side of the North-west arête, and learn enough to found more elaborate plans for exploring this side of the mountain should they turn
out to be necessary. Again we were fortunate in finding a good
camping ground, better even than the first, for the floor of this
shelf was grassy and soft, and as we were looking South across the
West Rongbuk Glacier we had the sun late as well as early. But we
were not completely happy. A Mummery tent may be well enough
in fair weather, though even then its low roof suggests a recumbent
attitude; it makes a poor dining-room, even for two men, and is a
cold shelter from snow. Moreover, the cold and draught discouraged our Primus stove—but I leave to the imagination of those
who have learned by experience the nausea that comes from the
paraffin fumes and one's dirty hands and all the mess that may be.
It was chiefly a question of incompetence, no doubt, but there was
no consolation in admitting that. In the morning, with the weather
still very thick and the snow lying about us we saw the error of our
ways. Is it not a first principle of mountaineering to be as comfortable as possible as long as one can? And how long should we require
for these operations in such weather? It was clear that our Second
Advanced Camp must be organised on a more permanent basis. On
the 9th therefore I went down to the base and moved it up on the
following day so as to be within reach of our present position by
one long march. The new place greatly pleased me; it was much
more sheltered than the lower site and the tents were pitched on flat
turf where a clear spring flowed out from the hillside and only a
quarter of an hour below the end of the glacier. Meanwhile Bullock
brought up the Whymper tents and more stores from the First
Advanced Camp, which was now established as a half-way house
with our big 80-feet tent standing in solemn grandeur to protect all
that remained there. On 10 July I was back at the Second Advanced
Camp and felt satisfied that the new arrangements, and particularly
the presence of our cook, would give us a fair measure of comfort.

But we were still unable to move next day. The snowfall during the night was the heaviest we had yet seen and continued into the next day. Probably the coolies were not sorry for a rest after some hard work; and we reckoned to make a long expedition so soon as the weather should clear. Towards evening on the 10th the clouds broke. Away to the South-west of us and up the glacier was the barrier range on the frontier of Nepal, terminated by one great mountain, Pumori, over 24,000 feet high. To the West Rongbuk Glacier they present the steepest slopes on which snow can lie; the crest above these slopes is surprisingly narrow and the peaks which it joins are fantastically shaped. This group of mountains, always beautiful and often in the highest degree impressive, was now to figure for our eyes as the principal in that oft-repeated drama which seems always to be a first night, fresh and full of wonder whenever we are present to watch it. The clinging curtains were rent and swirled aside and closed again, lifted and lowered and flung wide at last; sunlight broke through with sharp shadows and clean edges revealed—and we were there to witness the amazing spectacle. Below the terrible mountains one white smooth island rose from the quiet sea of ice and was bathed in the calm full light of the Western sun before the splendour failed.

With hopes inspired by the clearing views of this lovely evening, we started at 5.30 a.m. on 12 July to follow the glacier round to the South and perhaps enter the Western cwm. The glacier was a difficult problem. It looked easy enough to follow up the medial moraine to what we called the Island, a low mountain pushed out from the frontier ridge into the great sea of ice. But the way on Southwards from there would have been a gamble with the chances of success against us. We decided to cross the glacier directly to the South with a certainty that once we had reached the moraine on the other side we should have a clear way before us. It was exhilarating to set out again under a clear sky, and we were delighted to think that a large part of this task was accomplished when the sun rose full of warmth and cheerfulness. The far side was cut off by a stream of white ice, so narrow here that we expected with a little good fortune to get through it in perhaps half an hour. We entered it by a frozen stream leading into a bay with high white towers and ridges above us. A side door led through into a further bay which took us in the confidence of success almost through the maze. With some vigorous blows we cut our way up the final wall and then found ourselves on a crest overlooking the moraine with a sheer ice-precipice of about 200 feet below us.

The only hope was to come down again and work round to the right. Some exciting climbing and much hard work brought us at length to the foot of the cliffs and on the right side. The performance had taken us two and a half hours and it was nearly ten o'clock. Clouds had already come up to obscure the mountains, and from the point of view of a prolonged exploration the day was clearly lost. Our course now was to make the best of it and yet get back so early to camp that we could set forth again on the following day. We had the interest, after following the moraine to the corner where the glacier bends Southwards, of making our way into the middle of the ice and finding out how unpleasant it can be to walk on a glacier melted everywhere into little valleys and ridges and covered with fresh snow. We got back at 3 p.m.

On 13 July, determined to make good, we started at 4.15 a.m. With the knowledge gained on the previous day and the use of 250 feet of spare rope, we were able to find our way through the ice pinnacles and reached the far moraine in less than an hour and a half, and we had the further good fortune when we took to the snow to find it now in such good condition that we were able to walk on the surface without using our snow-shoes. As we proceeded up the slopes where the snow steepened the weather began to thicken and we halted at 8 a.m. in a thick mist with a nasty wind and some snow falling. It was a cold halt. We were already somewhat disillusioned about our glacier, which seemed to be much more narrow than was to be expected if it were really a high-road to the Western cwm, and as we went on with the wind blowing the snow into our faces so that nothing could be clearly distinguished we had the sense of a narrowing place and a perception of the even surface being broken up into large crevasses on one side and the other. At 9.30 we could go no further. For a few hundred yards we had been traversing a slope which rose above us on our left, and now coming out on to a little spur we stood peering down through the mist and knew ourselves to be on the edge of a considerable precipice. Not a single feature of the landscape around us was even faintly visible in the cloud. For a time we stayed on with the dim hope of better things and then reluctantly retired, baffled and bewildered.

Where had we been? It was impossible to know; but at least it was certain there was no clear way to the West side of Everest. We could only suppose that we had reached a col on the frontier of Nepal.

A further disappointment awaited us when we reached camp at 1 p.m. I had made a simple plan to ensure our supply of gobar[10] and rations from the base camp. The supplies had not come up and it was not the sort of weather to be without a fire for cooking.

I shall now proceed to quote my diary:

14 July A day of rest, but with no republican demonstrations. Very late breakfast after some snow in the night. Piquet after tiffin and again after dinner was very consoling. The little streams we found here on arrival are drying up; it seems that not much snow can have fallen higher.

15 July Started 6 a.m. to explore the glacier to West and North-west. A very interesting view just short of the Island; the South Peak appearing. Fifty minutes there for photos; then hurried on the hope of seeing more higher up and at a greater distance. It is really a dry glacier here but with snow frozen over the surface making many pitfalls. We had a good many wettings in cold water up to the knees. The clouds were just coming up as we halted on the medial moraine. I waited there in hope of better views, while Bullock took on the coolies. They put on snow-shoes for the first time and seemed to go very well in them. Ultimately I struggled across the glacier, bearing various burdens, to meet them as they came down on a parallel moraine. Snow-shoes seemed useful, but very awkward to leap in. Bullock went a long way up the glacier, rising very slightly towards the peak Cho-Uyo, 26,870 feet. Evidently there is a flat pass over into Nepal near this peak, but he did not quite reach it.

The topographical mystery centres about the West Peak. Is there an arête connecting this with the great rock peak South of Everest or is it joined up with the col we reached the day before yesterday? The shape of the West cwm and the question of its exit will be solved if we can answer these questions. Bullock and I are agreed that the glacier there has probably an exit on the Nepal side. It all remains extremely puzzling. We saw the North Col quite clearly today, and again the way up from there does not look difficult.

A finer day and quite useful. Chitayn[11] started out with us and went back. He appears to be seedy, but has been quite hopeless as Sirdar down in the base camp and is without authority. It is a great handicap having no one to look after things down there. Chitayn is returning to Tingri tomorrow. I hope he will cheer up again.

16 July I made an early start with two coolies at 2.45 a.m. and followed the medial moraine to the Island. Reached the near summit at sunrise about 5.30. Difficult to imagine anything more exciting than the clear view of all peaks. Those near me to the South-west quickly bathed in sun and those to the South and East showing me their dark faces. To the left of our col of 13 July a beautiful sharp peak stood in front of the gap between Everest and the North Peak, Changtse. Over this col I saw the North-west buttress of Everest hiding the lower half of the West face which must be a tremendous precipice of rock. The last summit of the South Peak, Lhotse, was immediately behind the shoulder; to the right (i.e. West)

Summit of Mount Everest and North Peak from the Island, West Rongbuk Glacier.

of it I saw a terrible arête stretching a long distance before it turned upwards in my direction and towards the West Peak. This mountain dropped very abruptly to the North, indicating a big gap on the far side of our col. There was the mysterious cwm lying in cold shadow long after the sun warmed me! But I now half understand it. The col under the Northwest buttress at the head of the Rongbuk Glacier is one entrance, and our col of 13 July, with how big a drop one knows not, another.

I stayed till 7 a.m. taking photos, a dozen plates exposed in all. The sky was heavy and a band of cloud had come across Everest before I left.

Back to breakfast towards 9 a.m. A pleasant morning collecting flowers, not a great variety but some delicious honey scents and an occasional cheerful blue poppy.

17 July More trouble with our arrangements. The Sirdar has muddled the rations and the day is wasted. However, the weather is bad, constant snow showers from 1 to 8 p.m., so that I am somewhat reconciled to this reverse.

18 July Yesterday's plan carried out—to move up a camp with light tents and make a big push over into the West cwm; eight coolies to carry the loads. But the loads have been too heavy. What can be cut out next time? I cannot see many unnecessary articles. Heavy snow showers fell as we came up and we had rather a cheerless encampment, but with much heaving of stones made good places for the tents. A glorious night before we turned in. Dark masses of cloud were gathered round the peak above us; below, the glacier was clear and many splendid mountains were half visible. The whole scene was beautifully lit by a bright moon.

19 July Started 3 a.m.; still some cloud, particularly to the West. The moon just showed over the mountains in that direction which cast their strange black shadows on the snow-field. One amazing black tooth was standing up against the moonlight. No luck on the glacier and we had to put on snow-shoes at once. An exciting walk. I so much feared the cloud would spoil all. It was just light enough to get on without lanterns after the moon went down. At dawn almost everything was covered, but not by heavy clouds. Like guilty creatures of darkness surprised by the light they went scattering away as we came up and the whole scene opened out. The North ridge of Everest was clear and bright even before sunrise. We reached the col at 5 a.m., a fantastically beautiful scene; and we looked across into the West cwm at last, terribly cold and forbidding under the shadow of Everest. It was nearly an hour after sunrise before the sun hit the West Peak.

Mount Everest from the Rongbuk Glacier (nine miles north-west)

But another disappointment—it is a big drop about 1,500 feet to the glacier, and a hopeless precipice. I was hoping to get away to the left and traverse into the cwm; that too quite hopeless. However, we have seen this Western glacier and are not sorry we have not to go up it. It is terribly steep and broken. In any case work on this side could only be carried out from a base in Nepal, so we have done with the Western side. It was not a very likely chance that the gap between Everest and the South Peak could be reached from the West. From what we have seen now I do not much fancy it would be possible, even could one get up the glacier.

We saw a lovely group of mountains away to the South in Nepal. I wonder what they are and if anything is known about them. It is a big world!

* * *

With this expedition on July 19 our reconnaissance of these parts had ended. We proceeded at once to move down our belongings; on July 20 all tents and stores were brought down to the base camp and we had said good-bye to the West Rongbuk Glacier.

So far as we were concerned with finding a way up the mountain, little enough had been accomplished; and yet our growing view of the mountain had been steadily leading to one conviction. If ever the mountain were to be climbed, the way would not lie along the whole length of any one of its colossal ridge. Progress could only be made along comparatively easy ground, and anything like a prolonged sharp crest or a series of towers would inevitably bar the way simply by the time which would be required to overcome such obstacles. But the North arête coming down to the gap between Everest and the North Peak, Changtse, is not of this character. From the horizontal structure of the mountain there is no excrescence of rock pinnacles in this part and the steep walls of rock which run across the North face are merged with it before they reach this part, which is comparatively smooth and continuous, a bluntly rounded edge. We had still to see other parts of the mountain, but already it seemed unlikely that we would find more favourable ground than this. The great question before us now was to be one of access. Could the North Col be reached from the East and how could we attain this point?

At the very moment when we reached the base camp, I received a note from Colonel Howard-Bury telling us that his departure from Tingri was fixed for 23 July and that he would be sleeping at Chöbu in the valley below us two days later on his way to Kharta. It was now an obvious plan to synchronise our movements with his.

Besides the branch which we had already explored the Rongbuk Glacier has yet another which joins the main stream from the East about 10 miles from Everest. It had always excited our curiosity, and I now proposed to explore it in the initial stages of a journey across the unknown ridges and valleys which separated us from Kharta. I calculated that we should want eight days' provisions, and that we should just have time to organise a camp in advance and start on the 25th with a selected party, sending down the rest to join Howard-Bury. And it was an integral part of the scheme that on one of the intervening days I should ascend a spur to the North of the glacier where we proposed to march in order to obtain a better idea of this country to the East. But we were now in the thickest of the monsoon weather; the 21st and 22nd were both wet days and we woke on the 23rd to find snow all around us nearly a foot deep; it had come down as low as 16,000 feet. It was hardly the weather to cut ourselves adrift and wander among the uncharted spurs of Everest, and we thought of delaying our start. Further it transpired that our organisation was not running smoothly—it never did run smoothly so long as we employed, as an indispensable Sirdar, a whey-faced treacherous knave whose sly and calculated villainy too often, before it was discovered, deprived our coolies of their food, and whose acquiescence in his own illimitable incompetence was only less disgusting than his infamous duplicity. It was the hopeless sense that things were bound to go wrong if we trusted to this man's services—and we had no one else at that time through whom it was possible to order supplies from the natives—that turned the scale and spoilt the plan. Even so, in the natural course of events, I should have obtained my preliminary view. But on the night of the 22nd I received from Howard-Bury an extremely depressing piece of news, that all my photos taken with the quarter-plate camera had failed—for the good reason that the plates had been inserted back to front, a result of ignorance and misunderstanding. It was necessary as far as possible to repair this hideous error, and the next two days were spent in a photographic expedition. And so it came about that we saw no more until a much later date of the East Rongbuk Glacier. Had our plan been carried out even in the smallest part by a cursory survey of what lay ahead, I should not now have to tell a

story which is lamentably incomplete in one respect. For the East
Rongbuk Glacier is one way, and the obvious way when you see it,
to the North Col. It was discovered by Major Wheeler before ever
we saw it, in the course of his photographic survey; but neither he,
nor Bullock, nor I have ever traversed its whole length.

We should have attached more
importance, no doubt, in the
early stages of reconnaissance, to
the East Rongbuk Glacier had we
not been deceived in two ways by
appearances. It had been an early
impression left in my mind, at all
events, by what we saw from
Shiling, that a deep valley came
down to the East as the R.G.S.
map suggests, draining into the
Arun and having the North-east
arête of Everest as its right bank
at the start. Further, the head of
this valley seemed to be, as one

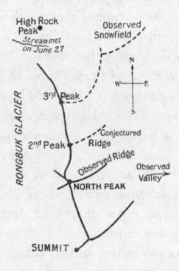

would expect, the gap between Everest and the first peak to the
North which itself has also an Eastern arm to form the left bank of
such a valley. The impression was confirmed not only by an excellent view from a hill above Ponglet (two days before Tingri and
about 35 miles North of Everest), but by all nearer and more recent
views of the mountains East of the Rongbuk Glacier. The idea that
a glacier running parallel to the Rongbuk started from the slopes of
Everest itself, and came so far to turn Westward in the end hardly
occurred to us at this time. From anything we had seen there was
no place for such a glacier, and it was almost unimaginable that the
great mountain range running North from the North Col, Chang
La, was in no part a true watershed. We saw the East Rongbuk
Glacier stretching away to the East and perceived also a bay to the

South. But how, if this bay were of any importance, could the glacier stream be so small? We had found it too large to cross, it is true, late in the afternoon of our first expedition, but only just too large; and again it seems now an unbelievable fact that so large an area of ice should give so small a volume of water. The glacier streams are remarkably small in all the country we explored, but this one far more surprisingly small than any other we saw.

It was some measure of consolation in these circumstances to make use of a gleam of fine weather. When the bad news arrived on July 22 about the failure of my photographs we had ceased to hear the raindrops pattering on the tent, but could feel well enough when we pushed up the roof that snow was lying on the outer fly. It was a depressing evening. I thought of the many wonderful occasions when I had caught the mountain as I thought just at the right moment, its moments of most lovely splendour—of all those moments that would never return and of the record of all we had seen which neither ourselves nor perhaps anyone else would ever see-again. I was not a cheerful companion. Moreover, from the back of my mind I was warned, even in the first despair of disappointment, that I should have to set out to repair the damage so far as I was able, and I hated the thought of this expedition. These were our days of rest after a month's high-living; we were off with one adventure and on with another; tents, stores, everything had been brought down to our base and we had said good-bye to the West Rongbuk Glacier. The clouds were still about us next morning and snow lay on the ground 9 inches deep. But by midday much of the snow had melted at our level and the clouds began to clear. At 2 p.m. we started up with the Mummery tents and stores for one night. I made my way with one coolie to a spot some little distance above our First Advanced Camp. As we pushed up the stormy hillside the last clouds gathered about Everest, and lingering in the deep North cwm were dispersed and the great white-mantled mountains lay all clear in the light of a glorious evening. Before we

raced down to join Bullock my first dozen plates had been duly
exposed; whatever the balance of hopes and fears for a fine morning to-morrow something had been done already to make good.

Summit of Mount Everest and South Peak, from the Rongbuk Glacier.

My ultimate destination was the Island which I had found before
to command some of the most splendid and most instructive views.
I was close up under the slopes of this little mountain before sunrise next morning. It has rarely been my lot to experience in the
course of a few hours so much variety of expectation, of disappointment and of hope deferred, before the issue is decided. A pall
of cloud lying like a blanket above the glacier was no good omen
after the clear weather; as the sun got up a faint gleam on the ice
encouraged me to go on; presently the grey clouds began to move
and spread in all directions until I was enveloped and saw nothing.
Suddenly the frontier crest came out and its highest peak towering
fantastically above me; I turned about and saw to the West and
Northwest the wide glacier in the sun—beyond it Gyachung Bang

and Cho-Uyo, 26,870 to 25,990 feet: but Everest remained hidden, obscured by an impenetrable cloud. I watched the changing shadows on the white snow and gazed helplessly into the grey mass continually rolled up from Nepal into the deep hollow beyond the glacier head. But a breeze came up from the East; the curtain was quietly withdrawn; Everest and the South Peak stood up against the clear blue sky. The camera was ready and I was satisfied. A few minutes later the great cloud rolled back and I saw no more.

Meanwhile Bullock had not been idle. He paid a visit to the North cwm, more successful than mine in July, for he reached the pass leading over into Nepal under the Northwest wile and had perfectly clear views of Chang La, of which he brought back some valuable photos. But perhaps an even greater satisfaction than reckoning the results of what we both felt was a successful day was ours, when we listened in our tents that evening at the base camp to the growling of thunder and reflected that the fair interval already ended had been caught and turned to good account.

In snow and sleet and wind next morning, July 25, our tents were struck. We turned our backs on the Rongbuk Glacier and hastened along the path to Chöbuk. The valley was somehow changed as we came down, and more agreeable to the eye. Presently I discovered the reason. The grass had grown on the hillside since we went up. We were coming down to summer green.

6c
The Eastern Approach

The new base at Kharta established by Colonel Howard-Bury at the end of July was well suited to meet the needs of climbers, and no less agreeable, I believe, to all members of the Expedition. At the moderate elevation of 12,300 feet and in an almost ideal climate, where the air was always warm but never hot or stuffy, where the sun shone brightly but never fiercely, and clouds floated about the hills and brought moisture from the South, but never too much rain, here the body could find a delicious change when tired of the discipline of high-living, and in a place so accessible to traders from Nepal could easily be fed with fresh food. But perhaps after life in the Rongbuk Valley, with hardly a green thing to look at and too much of the endless unfriendly stone-shoots and the ugly waste of glaciers, and even after visions of sublime snow-beauty, a change was more needed for the mind. It was a delight to be again in a land of flowery meadows and trees and crops; to look into the deep green gorge only a mile away where the Arun goes down into Nepal was to be reminded of a rich vegetation and teeming life, a contrast full of pleasure with Nature's niggardliness in arid, wind-swept Tibet; and the forgotten rustle of wind in the willows came back as a soothing sound full of grateful memories, banishing the least thought of disagreeable things.

The Kharta base, besides, was convenient for our reconnaissance. Below us a broad glacier stream joined the Arun above the gorge; it was the first met with since we had left the Rongbuk stream; it came down from the West and therefore, presumably, from Everest. To follow it up was an obvious plan as the next stage in our activities. After four clear days for idleness and reorganisation at Kharta we set forth again on 2 August with this object. The valley of our glacier stream would lead us, we supposed, to the mountain; in two days, perhaps, we should see Chang La ahead of us. A local head-man provided by the jongpen and entrusted with the task of leading us to Chomolungma would show us where it might be necessary to cross the stream and, in case the valley forked, would ensure us against a bad mistake.

The start of this day was not propitious. We had enjoyed the sheltered ease at Kharta; the coolies were dilatory and unwilling; the distribution of loads was muddled; there was much discontent about rations, and our Sirdar was no longer trusted by the men. At a village where we stopped to buy tsampa some three miles up the valley I witnessed a curious scene. As the tsampa was sold it had to be measured. The Sirdar on his knees before a large pile of fine ground flour was ladling it into a bag with a disused Quaker Oats tin. Each measure-full was counted by all the coolies standing round in a circle; they were making sure of having their full ration. Nor was this all; they wanted to see as part of their supplies, not only tsampa and rice, but tea, sugar, butter, cooking fat and meat on the Army scale. This was a new demand altogether beyond the bargain made with them. The point, of course, had to be clearly made, that for their so-called luxuries I must be trusted to do my best with the surplus money (100 tankas or thereabouts) remaining over from their allowances after buying the flour and rice. These luxury supplies were always somewhat of a difficulty; the coolies had been very short of such things on the Northern side—we had no doubt

Pethang-She.

that some of the ration money had found its way into the Sirdar's pockets. It would be possible, we hoped, to prevent this happening again. But even so the matter was not simple. What the coolies wanted was not always to be bought, or at the local price it was too expensive. On this occasion a bountiful supply of chillies solved our difficulty. After too many words, and not all in the best temper, the sight of so many of the red, bright, attractive chillies prevailed; at length my orders were obeyed; the coolies took up their loads and we started off again.

With so much dissatisfaction in the air it was necessary for Bullock and me to drive rather than lead the party. In a valley where there are many individual farms and little villages, the coolies' path is well beset with pitfalls and with gin. Without discipline the Sahib might easily find himself at the end of a day's march with perhaps only half his loads. It was a slow march this day; we had barely accomplished eight miles, when Bullock and I with the hindmost came round a shoulder on the right bank about 4 p.m. and found the tents pitched on a grassy shelf and looking up a valley where a stream came in from our left. The Tibetan head-man and his Tibetan coolies who were carrying some of our loads had evidently no intention of going further, and after some argument I was content to make the stipulation that if the coolies (our own as well as the Tibetans) chose to encamp after half a day's march, they should do a double march next day.

The prospect was far from satisfactory: we were at a valley junction of which we had heard tell, and the head-man pointed the way to the left. Here indeed was a valley, but no glacier stream. It was a pleasant green nullah covered with rhododendrons and juniper, but presented nothing that one may expect of an important valley. Moreover, so far as I could learn, there were no villages in this direction: I had counted on reaching one that night with the intention of buying provisions, more particularly goats and butter. Where were we going and what should we find? The head-man announced that it would take us five more days to reach Chomolungma: he was told that he must bring us there in two, and so the matter was left.

If the coolies behaved badly on this first day, they certainly made up for it on the second. The bed of the little valley which we now followed rose steeply ahead of us, and the path along the hill slopes on its left bank soon took us up beyond the rhododendrons. We came at last for a midday halt to the shores of a lake. It was the first I had seen in the neighbourhood of Everest; a little blue lake, perhaps 600 yards long, set on a flat shelf up there among the clouds and rocks, a sympathetic place harbouring a wealth of little rock plants on its steep banks; and as our present height by the aneroid was little less than 17,000 feet, we were assured that on this Eastern side of Everest we should find Nature in a gentler mood. But we were not satisfied with our direction; we were going too much to the South. Through the mists we had seen nothing to help us. For a few moments some crags had appeared to the left looming surprisingly big; but that was our only peep, and it told us nothing. Perhaps from the pass ahead of us we should have better fortune.

At the Langma La when we reached it we found ourselves to be well 4,000 feet above our camp of the previous night. We had followed a track, but not always a smooth one, and as we stayed in hopes of a clearing view, I began to wonder whether the Tibetan coolies would manage to arrive with their loads; they were notably less strong than our Sherpas and yet had been burdened with the wet heavy tents. Meanwhile we saw nothing above our own height. We had hoped that once our col was crossed we should bear more directly Westward again; but the Tibetan head-man when he came up with good news of his coolies, pointed our way across a deep valley below us, and the direction of his pointing was nearly due South. Everest, we imagined, must be nearly due West of Kharta, and our direction at the end of this second day by a rough dead reckoning would be something like South-west. We were more than ever mystified. Fortunately our difficulties with the coolies seemed to be ended. Two of our own men stayed at the pass to relieve the Tibetans of the tents and bring them quickly on. Grumblings had subsided in friendliness, and all marched splendidly on this day. They were undepressed with the gloomy circumstance of again encamping in the rain.

In the Sahibs' tent that night there took place a long and fragmentary conversation with the head-man, our Sirdar acting as interpreter. We gained one piece of information: there were two Chomolungmas. It was not difficult to guess that, if Everest were one, the other must be Makalu. We asked to be guided to the furthest Chomolungma.

The morning of 4 August was not more favourable to our reconnaissance. We went down steeply to the valley bed, crossed a stream and a rickety bridge, and wound on through lovely meadows and much dwarf rhododendron till we came to the end of a glacier and mounted by its left bank. Towards mid-day the weather showed signs of clearing; suddenly on our left across the glacier we saw gigantic precipices looming through the clouds. We guessed they must belong in some way to Makalu. We were told that this was the first Chomolungma, while the valley we were now following would lead us to the other. It was easy to conclude that one valley, this one, must come up on the North side of Makalu all the way to Everest. But we saw no more. In a few moments the grey clouds blowing swiftly up from below had enveloped us, rain began to fall heavily, and when eventually we came to broad meadows above the glaciers, where yaks were grazing and Tibetan tents were pitched, we were content to stop. At least we should have the advantage here of good butter and cream from this dairy farm. There was indeed no point in going farther; we had no desire to run our heads against the East face of Everest; we must now wait for a view.

The weather signs were decidedly more hopeful as I looked out of our tent next morning, and we decided at once to spend the day in some sort of reconnaissance up the valley. Presently away at the head of it we saw the clouds breaking about the mountainsides. Everest itself began to clear; the great North-east arête came out, cutting the sky to the right; and little by little the whole Eastern face was revealed to us.

As I recall now our first impression of the amazing scenery around us, I seem chiefly to remember the fresh surprise and vivid delight which, for all we had seen before, seemed a new sensation. Even the map of the Kama Valley, now that we have it, may stir the imagination. Besides Everest itself the crest of the South Peak, 28,000 feet high, and its prodigious South-east shoulder overlook the Western end; while Makalu, 12 miles from Everest, thrusts out Northwards a great arm and another peak to choke the exit; so that whereas the frontier ridge from Everest to Makalu goes in a South-easterly direction, the Kangshung Glacier in the main valley runs nearly due East. In this spacious manner three of the five highest summits in the world overlook the Kama Valley.

And we now saw a scene of magnificence and splendour even more remarkable than the facts suggest. Among all the mountains I have seen, and, if we may judge by photographs, all that ever have been seen, Makalu is incomparable for its spectacular and rugged grandeur. It was significant to us that the astonishing precipices rising above us on the far side of the glacier as we looked across from our camp, a terrific awe-inspiring sweep of snowbound rocks, were the sides not so much of an individual mountain, but rather of a gigantic bastion or outwork defending Makalu. At the broad head of the Kama Valley the two summits of Everest are enclosed between the North-east arête and the South-east arête bending round from the South Peak; below them is a basin of tumbled ice well marked by a number of moraines and receiving a series of tributaries pouring down between the buttresses which support the mountain faces in this immense cirque. Perhaps the astonishing charm and beauty here lie in the complications half hidden behind a mask of apparent simplicity, so that one's eye never tires of following up the lines of the great arêtes, of following down the arms pushed out from their great shoulders, and of following along the broken edge of the hanging glacier covering the upper half of this Eastern face of Everest so as to determine at one point after another its relation with the buttresses below and with their abutments against the rocks which it covers. But for me the most magnificent and sublime in mountain scenery can be made lovelier by some more tender touch; and that, too, is added here. When all is said about Chomolungma, the Goddess Mother of the World, and about Chomo Uri, the Goddess of the Turquoise Mountain, I come back to the valley, the valley bed itself, the broad pastures, where our tents lay, where cattle grazed and where butter was made, the little stream we followed up to the valley head, wandering along its well-turfed banks under the high moraine, the few rare plants, saxifrages, gentians and primulas, so well watered there, and a soft, familiar blueness in the air which even here may charm us. Though I bow to the goddesses I cannot forget at their feet a gentler spirit than theirs, a little shy perhaps, but constant in the changing winds and variable moods of mountains and always friendly.

The deviation from our intended line of approach involved by entering the Kama Valley was not one which we were likely to regret. In so far as our object was to follow up a glacier to the North Col we were now on the wrong side of a watershed. A spur of mountains continues Eastwards from the foot of Everest's North-east arête; these were on our right as we looked up the Kama Valley; the glacier of our quest must lie on the far side of them. But the pursuit of this glacier was not our sole object. We had also to examine both the East face and North-east arête of our mountain and determined the possibilities of attack on this side. A plan was now made to satisfy us in all ways. We chose as our objective a conspicuous snowy summit, Carpo-ri, on the watershed and apparently the second to the East from the foot of the North-east arête. Could we climb it we should not only see over into the valley North of us and

Summit of Makalu.

up to Chang La itself, we hoped, but also examine, from the point most convenient for judging the steepness of its slopes, the whole of the Eastern side of Mount Everest.

On 6 August the Whymper tents were taken up, and a camp was made under a moraine at about 17,500 feet, where a stream flows quietly through a flat space before plunging steeply down into the valley. In this sheltered spot we bid defiance to the usual snowstorm of the afternoon; perhaps as night came on and snow was still falling we were vaguely disquieted, but we refused to believe in anything worse than the heavens' passing spite, and before we put out our candles the weather cleared. We went out into the keen air; it was a night of early moons. Mounting a little rise of stones and faintly crunching under our feet the granular atoms of fresh fallen snow we were already aware of some unusual loveliness in the moment and the scenes. We were not kept waiting for the supreme effects; the curtain was withdrawn. Rising from the bright mists Mount Everest above us was imminent, vast, incalculable—no fleeting apparition of elusive dream-form: nothing could have been more set and permanent, steadfast like Keats's star, 'in lone splendour hung aloft the night', a watcher of all the nights, diffusing, it seemed universally, an exalted radiance.

It is the property of all that is most sublime in mountain scenery to be uniquely splendid, or at least to seem so, and it is commonly the fate of the sublime in this sort very soon to be mixed with what is trivial. Not infrequently we had experience of wonderful moments; it is always exciting to spend a night under the star. And such a situation may be arranged quite comfortably; lying with his head but just within the tent a man has but to stir in his sleep to see, at all events, half the starry sky. Then perhaps thoughts come tumbling from the heavens and slip in et the tent-door; his dozing is an ecstasy: until, at length, the alarm-watch sounds; and after? ... Mean considerations din it all away, all that delight. On the morning of August 7 the trivial, with us, preponderated. Something more than the usual inertia reigned in our frozen camp at 2 a.m. The cook was feeling unwell; the coolies prolonged their minutes of grace after the warning shout, dallied with the thought of meeting the cold air, procrastinated, drew the blankets more closely round them, and— snored once more. An expedition over the snow to the outlying tents by a half-clad Sahib, who expects to enjoy at least the advantage of withdrawing himself at the last moment from the friendly down-bag, is calculated to disturb the recumbency of others; and a kick-off in this manner to the day's work is at all events exhilarating. The task of extricating our frozen belongings, where they lay and ought not to have lain, was performed with alacrity if not with zeal; feet did not loiter over slippery boulders as we mounted the moraine, and in spite of the half-hour lost, or gained, we were well up by sunrise. Even before the first glimmer of dawn the snow-mantled, slumbering monsters around us had been somehow touched to life by a faint blue light showing their form and presence—a light that changed as the day grew to a pale yellow on Everest and then to a bright blue-grey before it flamed all golden as the sun hit the summit and the shadow crept perceptibly down the slope until the whole mountain stood bare and splendid hi the morning glory. With some premonition of what was in store for us we had already halted to enjoy the scene, and I was able to observe exactly how the various ridges and summits caught the sun. It was remarkable that while Everest was never, for a moment, pink, Makalu was tinged with the redder shades, and the colour of the sky in that direction was a livid Chinese blue red-flushed. Its bearing from us was about South-east by South, and its distance nearly twice that of Everest, which lay chiefly to the South-west.

The first crux of the expedition before us would evidently be the ascent of a steep wall up to the conspicuous col lying East of our mountain. The least laborious way was offered by an outcrop of rocks. The obstacle looked decidedly formidable and the coolies had little or no experience of rock-climbing. But it proved a pleasure reminiscent of many good moments once again to be grasping firm granite and to be encouraging novices to tread delicately by throwing down an occasional stone to remind them of the perils of clumsy movements. The coolies, as usual, were apt pupils, and after agreeable exertions and one gymnastic performance we all reached the col at 9 a.m. with no bleeding scalps.

We had already by this hour taken time to observe the great Eastern face of Mount Everest, and more particularly the lower edge of the hanging glacier; it required but little further gazing to be convinced—to know that almost everywhere the rocks below must be exposed to ice falling from this glacier; that if, elsewhere, it might be possible to climb up, the performance would be too arduous, would take too much time and would lead to no convenient platform; that, in short, other men, less wise, might attempt this way if they would, but, emphatically, it was not for us.

Our interest was rather in the other direction. We had now gained the watershed. Below us on the far side was a glacier flowing East, and beyond it two important rock peaks, which we at once suspected must be two triangulated points each above 23,000 feet. Was this at last the valley observed so long ago from the hill above Shiling, more than 50 miles away, to point up towards the gap between Changtse and Everest? As yet we could not say. The head of the glacier was out of sight behind the Northern slopes of our mountain. We must ascend further, probably to its summit, to satisfy our curiosity to see, we hoped, Changtse and its relation to this glacier, and perhaps the Chang La of our quest.

The task before us was not one which had suggested from a dis-

South-East Ridge of Mount Everest from above the 20,000 foot camp, Kharta Valley.

tant view any serious difficulties. The angle of sight from our break-fast-place on the col to the next white summit West of us was certainly not very steep. But no continuous ridge would lead us upwards. The East face in front of us and the South face to our left presented two bands of fortification, crowned each by a flat emplacement receding a considerable distance, before the final cone. We knew already that the snow's surface, despite a thin crust, could not hold us, and counted on snow-shoes to save labour at the gentler angles. But the escarpments in front of us were imposing. The first yielded to a frontal attack pushed home with a proper after-breakfast vigour. The second when we reached it was a more formidable obstacle. The steepness of the Eastern slope was undeniable and forbidding and the edge of its junction with the South side was defined by a cornice. On that side, however, lay the only hope.

We had first to traverse a broad gully. The powdery snow lay deep; we hesitated on the brink. Here, if anywhere, the unmelted powdery substance was likely to avalanche. Confidence was restored in sufficient measure by contemplating an island of rock. Here lay a solution. By the aid of its sound anchorage the party was secured across the dangerous passage. With his rope adequately belayed by a coolie, though the manner was hardly professional, the leader hewed at the cornice above his head, fixed a fist-and-axe hold in the crest and struggled over. Such performances are not accomplished at heights above 20,000 feet without the feeling that something has been done. Appearances suggested the necessity of establishing the whole party firmly above the cornice before proceeding many steps upward, and the first man had the diversion of observing at his leisure the ungraceful attitudes and explosive grunts of men strong indeed, but unaccustomed to meeting this kind of obstacle. But with the usual menace of clouds, which even now were filling the head of the Kama Valley, it was no season for delay; and it was no place to be treated lightly. The angle was quite as steep as we liked;

on the slopes to our left again we should evidently be exposed to
the danger of an avalanche. It was necessary to avoid treading on
our frail cornice and no less important to keep near the edge. Here
a foot of powdery snow masked a disintegrated substance of loose
ice. Nothing less than a vigorous swinging blow had any other
effect than to bury the pick and require a four-fold effort to pull it
out again. Luckily one or even two such blows usually sufficed to
make a firm step. But 400 feet of such work seemed an ample quantity. It was a relief at length to reach level snow, to don our rackets
again and to follow a coolie bursting with energy now sent first to
tread a path. At 12.15 p.m. we reached the far edge of this flat
shoulder lying under the final slopes of our mountain and at the
most 500 feet below the summit.

No one without experience of the problem could guess how difficult it may be to sit down on a perfectly flat place with snowshoes
strapped to the feet. To squat is clearly impossible; and if the feet
are pushed out in front the projection behind the heel tends to tilt
the body backwards so that the back is strained in the mere effort
to sit without falling. The remedy of course is to take off the snow-
shoes; but the human mountaineer after exhausting efforts is too
lazy for that at an elevation of 21,000 feet. He prefers not to sit; he
chooses to lie—in the one convenient posture under the circumstances—flat upon his back and with his toes and snow-shoes
turned vertically upwards. On this occasion the majority of the
party without more ado turned up their toes.

The situation, however, was one of the greatest interest. We were
still separated from Mount Everest by a spur at our own height
turning Northwards from the foot of the North-east arête and by
the bay enclosed between this and its continuation Eastward to
which our mountain belonged. But the distance from the North-
east arête was small enough and we were now looking almost directly up its amazing crest. If any doubts remained at this time as to that
line of attack, they now received a coup de grace. Not only was the

crest itself seen to be both sharp and steep, suggesting an almost infinite labour, but the slopes on either hand appeared in most places an impracticable alternative; and leading up to the great rock towers of the North-east shoulder, the final section, the point of a cruel sickle appeared effectually to bar further progress should any-one have been content to spend a week or so on the lower parts. To discern so much required no prolonged study; to the right (North) the country was more intricate. The summit of Changtse was even-tually revealed, as the clouds cleared of, beyond, apparently a long way beyond, the crest of the spur in front of us. To the extreme right, looking past the final slopes of the white cone above us, was a more elevated skyline and below it the upper part of the glacier, the lower end of which we had seen earlier in the day descending Eastward. But its extreme limit was not quite visible. We had still to ask the question as to where exactly it lay. Could this glacier con-ceivably proceed in an almost level course up to Chang La itself? Or was it cut off much nearer to us by the high skyline which we saw beyond it? Was it possible, as in the second case must be, that this skyline was continuous with the East arête of Changtse, the whole forming the left bank of the glacier? If no answer was absolutely certain, the probability at least was all on one side—on the wrong

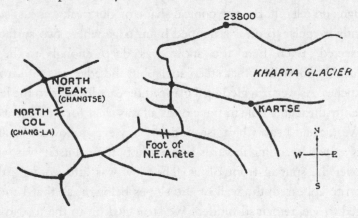

Diagram showing that the Kharta Glacier does not lead to the North Col.

side alike for our present and our future plans. We could hardly doubt that the glacier-head lay not far away under Chang La, but here near at hand under another col; beyond this must be the glacier of our quest, turning East, as presumably it must turn beyond the skyline we saw now, and beyond the rock peaks which we had observed to the North of us when first we reached the watershed.

One more effort was now required so that we might see a little more. Chang La itself was still invisible. Might we not see it from the summit of our mountain? And was it not in any case an attractive summit? An examination of the various pairs of upturned toes where the prostrate forms were still grouped grotesquely in the snow was not encouraging. But the most vigorous of the coolies was with us, Nyima, a sturdy boy of eighteen, who from the very start of the Expedition had consistently displayed a willing spirit in every emergency. To my demand for volunteers he responded immediately, and soon persuaded a second coolie, Dasno, who had been going very strongly on this day, to accompany him. As the three of us started off the clouds suddenly boiled up from below and enveloped us completely. A few minutes brought us to the foot of the steepest slopes; we took off our snow-shoes and crossed a bergschrund, wading up to our thighs. Dasno had already had enough and fell out. But the conical shape of our peak was just sufficiently irregular to offer a defined blunt edge where two surfaces intersected. Even here the snow was deep enough to be a formidable obstacle at that steep angle; but the edge was safe from avalanches. As we struggled on I glanced repeatedly away to the left. Presently through a hole in the clouds all was clear for a moment to the West; again I saw Changtse, and now my eyes followed the line of its arête descending towards Everest until the col itself was visible over the spur in front of us. The view was little enough; the mere rim appeared; the wall or the slopes below it, all that I most wanted to see, remained hidden. We struggled on to the top, in all nearly an hour's work of the most exhausting kind. The reward was in the beauty of the spot, the faintly defined edges of clean snow and the convex surfaces bent slightly back from the steepness on every side to form the most graceful summit I have seen. To the North-east we saw clearly for a minute down the glacier. The rest was cloud, a thin veil, but all too much, inexorably hiding from us Changtse and Chang La.

A disappointment? Perhaps. But that sort of suffering cannot be prolonged in a mind sufficiently interested. Possibly it is never a genuine emotion; rather an automatic reaction after too sanguine hope. And such hopes had no part in our system. We counted on nothing. Days as we found them were not seldom of the disappointing kind; this one had been of the best, remarkably clear and fine. If we were baffled that was no worse than we expected. To be bewildered was all in the game. But our sensation was something beyond bewilderment. We felt ourselves to be foiled. We were unpleasantly stung by this slap in the face. We had indeed solved all doubts as to the East face and North-east arête, and had solved them quickly. But the way to Chang La, which had seemed almost within our grasp, had suddenly eluded us, and had escaped, how far we could not tell. Though its actual distance from our summit might be short, as indeed it must be, the glacier of our quest appeared now at the end of a receding vista; and this was all our prospect.

Our next plans were made on the descent. With the relaxation of physical effort the feeling of dazed fatigue wears off and a mind duly strung to activity may work well enough. The immediate object was to reach our tents not too late to send a coolie down to the base camp the same evening; on the following morning a reinforcement of four men would enable us to carry down all our loads with sufficient ease, and with no delay we should move the whole party along the next stage back towards Langma La—and thus save a day. The main idea was simple. It still seemed probable that the elusive glacier drained ultimately Eastwards, in which case its waters must flow into the Kharta stream; thither we had now to retrace our steps and follow up the main valley as we had originally intended; it might be necessary to investigate more valleys than one, but there sooner or later a way would be found. Only, time was short. At the earliest we could be back in the Kharta Valley on 9 August. By 20 August I reckoned the preliminary reconnaissance should come to an end, if we were to have sufficient time before the beginning of September for rest and reorganisation at Kharta—and such was the core of our plan.

These projects left out of account an entirely new factor. In the early stages of the reconnaissance I had taken careful note of the party's health. One or two of the coolies had quickly fallen victims to the high altitudes; but the rest seemed steadily to grow stronger. Nothing had so much surprised us as the rapid acclimatisation of the majority, and the good effects, so far as they appeared, of living in high camps. Both Bullock and myself left the Rongbuk Valley feeling as fit as we could wish to feel. All qualms about our health had subsided. For my part I was a confirmed optimist, and never imagined for myself the smallest deviation from my uniform standard of health and strength. On 7 August, as we toiled over the névé in the afternoon, I felt for the first time a symptom of weariness beyond muscular fatigue and beyond the vague lassitude of mountain-sickness. By the time we reached the moraine I had a bad headache. In the tent at last I was tired and shivering and there spent a fevered night. The next morning broke with undeniable glory. A photograph of our yesterday's conquest must be obtained. I dragged myself and the quarter-plate camera a few steps up to the crest of the moraine—only to find that a further peregrination of perhaps 300 yards would be necessary for my purpose: and 300 yards was more than I could face. I was perforce content with less interesting exposures and returned to breakfast with the dismal knowledge that for the moment at all events I was *hors de combat*. We learned a little later that Colonel Howard-Bury had arrived the night before in our base camp. It was easily decided to spend the day there with him—the day I had hoped to save; after the long dragging march down the green way, which on the ascent had been so pleasant with butterflies and flowers, I was obliged to spend it in bed.

Three days later, on 11 August, our tents were pitched in a sheltered place well up the Kharta Valley, at a height of about 16,500 feet. Two tributary streams had been passed by, the first coming in from the North as being clearly too small to be of consequence, and the second from the South, because wherever its source might be, it could not be far enough to the North. Ahead of us we had seen that the valley forked; we must follow the larger stream and then no doubt we should come soon enough to the glacier of our quest and be able at last to determine whether it would serve us to approach Chang La. 12 August, a day of necessary idleness after three long marches, was spent by the coolies in collecting fuel, of which we were delighted to observe a great abundance, rhododendron and gobar all about us, and, only a short way down the valley, the best we could hope for, juniper. The last march had been too much for me, and again I was obliged to keep my bed with a sore throat and swollen glands.

It seemed certain that the next two days must provide the climax or anticlimax of our whole reconnaissance. The mystery must surely now be penetrated and the most important discovery of all be made. A competition with my companion for the honour of being first was, I hope, as far from my thoughts as ever it had been. From the start Bullock and I had shared the whole campaign and worked and made our plans together, and neither for a moment had envied the other the monopoly of a particular adventure. Nevertheless, after all that had passed, the experience of being left out at the finish would not be agreeable to me; I confess that not to be in at the death after leading the hunt so long was a bitter expectation. But the hunt must not be stopped, and on the morning of 13 August, from the ungrateful comfort of my sleeping-bag, I waved farewell to Bullock. How many days would he be absent before he came to tell his story, and what sort of story would it be? Would he know for certain that the way was found? Or how much longer would our doubts continue?

It was impossible to stay in bed with such thoughts, and by the middle of the morning I was sitting in the sun to write home my dismal tale. A hint from one of the coolies interrupted my meditations; I looked round and now saw, to my great surprise and unfeigned delight, the approaching figure of Major Morshead. I had long been hoping that he might be free to join us; and he arrived at the due moment to cheer my present solitude, to strengthen the party, and to help us when help was greatly needed. Moreover, he brought from Wollaston for my use a medical dope; stimulated by the unusual act of drug-taking, or possibly by the drug itself, I began to entertain a hope for the morrow, a feeling incommunicably faint but distinguishably a hope.

Meanwhile Bullock, though he had not started early, had got off soon enough in the morning to pitch his tents if all went well some hours before dark, and in all probability at least so far up as to be within view of the glacier snout. As the night was closing in a coolie was observed running down the last steep sandy slope to our camp. He brought a chit from Bullock: 'I can see up the glacier ahead of me and it ends in another high pass. I shall get to the pass tomorrow morning if I can, and ought to see our glacier over it. But it looks, after all, as though the most unlikely solution is the right one and the glacier goes out into the Rongbuk Valley.'

Into the Rongbuk Valley! We had discussed the possibility. The glacier coming in there from the East remained unexplored. But even if we left out of account all that was suggested by the East arête of Changtse and other features of this country, there remained the unanswerable difficulty about the stream, the little stream which we had but just failed to cross in the afternoon of our first expedition. How could so little water drain so large an area of ice as must exist on this supposition?

In any case we were checked again. The mystery deepened. And though the interest might increase, the prospect of finding a way to Chang La, with the necessary margin of time before the end of the month, was still receding, and, whether or not the unexpected should turn out to be the truth, the present situation suggested the unpleasant complication of moving our base once more somewhere away to the North.

On the following day with the gathering energy of returning health I set forth with Morshead: we walked in a leisurely fashion up the valley rejected by Bullock and had the surprising good fortune of a clear sky until noon. I soon decided that we were looking up the glacier where we had looked down on the 7th, as Bullock too had decided on the previous day: at the head of it was a high snow col and beyond that the tip of Changtse. What lay between them? If a combe existed there, as presumably it did, the bed of it must be high: there could hardly be room, I thought, for a very big drop on the far side of the col. Might not this, after all, be a sufficiently good approach, a more convenient way perhaps than to mount the glacier from its foot, wherever that might be? The near col, so far as I could judge, should easily be reached from this side. Why not get to the col and find out what lay beyond it? The time had come to abandon our object of finding the foot of a glacier in order to follow it up; for we could more easily come to the head of it and if necessary follow it down.

I was sanguine about this new plan, which seemed to have good prospects of success and might obviate the difficulties and inconvenience of shifting the base (possibly again to the Rongbuk side, which I had no desire to revisit) and, as I still felt far from fit, I was in some hopes now that two more days would bring us to the end of our present labours. Bullock very readily agreed to the proposal. He brought no positive information from the col which he had reached, though he inclined to the idea that the water crossed at Harlung on our journey to Kharta, a moderate stream, but perhaps too clear, might provide the solution of our problem. A fresh bone was now thrown into our stew. A letter arrived from Howard-Bury with an enclosure from Wheeler, a sketch map of what he had seen more particularly East of the Rongbuk Glacier, on which the Eastern branch, with its Western exit, was clearly marked where we now know it to be. It was, unfortunately, a very rough map, professedly nothing more, and was notably wrong in some respects about which we had accurate knowledge. We were not yet convinced that the head of the East Rongbuk Glacier was really situated under the slopes of Everest, and not perhaps under the Eastern arm of Changtse. Still, we had some more pickings to digest. Our business was to reach the nearer pass, and I felt sure that once we had looked over it to the other side whatever doubts remained could be cleared up in subsequent discussion with Wheeler. Meanwhile, I hoped, we should have discovered one way to Chang La, and a sufficiently good one.

It took us in the sequel not two but four days to reach the pass which was ultimately known as Lhakpa La (Windy Gap). The story may serve as a fair illustration of the sort of difficulty with which we had to contend. It was arranged on the 15th that we should meet Bullock's coolies at the divide in the valley; they were bringing down his camp and we could all go on together: but our messenger succeeded in collecting only half their number and much delay was caused in waiting for the others. From here we followed the Western stream, a stony and rather fatiguing walk of two hours or so (unladen) up to the end of the glacier, and then followed a moraine shelf on its left bank. I hoped we should find an easy way round to the obvious camping place we had previously observed from the Carpo-ri. But the shelf ended abruptly on steep stony slopes, clouds obscured our view, and after our misfortunes in the morning we were now short of time, so that it was necessary to stay where we were for the night. A thick layer of mist was still lying along the valley when we woke, and we could see nothing, but were resolved, nevertheless, to reach the col if possible. We went up, for the best chance of a view, to the crest of the hill above us, and followed it to the summit (6.30 a.m.). The view was splendid, and I took some good photographs; but the drop on the far side was more serious than our hopes had suggested. We tried to make the best of things by contouring and eventually halted for breakfast on the edge of the glacier a long way North of the direct line at 8.45 a.m. Before we went on we were again enveloped in mist, and after stumbling across the glacier in snow-shoes to the foot of an icefall, we turned back at 11 a.m. By that time we were a tired party and could not have reached the col; and even had we reached it, we should have seen nothing. Still we felt when we found our tents again that with all we had seen the day had not been lost, and we determined, before renewing our attempt on Lhakpa La, to push on the camp. There was still time to send a message down to the Sirdar so as to get up more coolies and supplies and move forward next day. From this higher camp we hoped that the col might be reached at an early hour, and in that case it would be possible for a party to cross it and descend the glacier on the other side.

The first coolies who came up in the morning brought a message from the Sirdar to the effect that supplies were short and he could send none up. The rations were calculated to last for another three days, but their distribution had been muddled. However, enough was subsequently sent up to carry us over into the next day, though it was necessary of course to abandon our project of a more distant reconnaissance. Our camp was happily established in the usual snowstorm. The weather, in fact, was not treating us kindly. Snow was falling in these days for about eight to ten hours on the average and we were relieved at last to see a fine morning.

On 18 August, with the low moon near setting, the three of us with one coolie set forth on the most critical expedition of our whole reconnaissance. Failure on this day must involve us in a lamentable delay before the party could again be brought up for the attack; at the earliest we should be able to renew the attempt four days later, and if in the end the way were not established here the whole prospect of the assault in September would be in jeopardy. We scaled the little cliff on to the glacier that morning with the full consciousness that one way or another it was an imperative necessity to reach the col. The first few steps on the glacier showed us what to expect; we sank in to our knees. The remedy was, of course, to put on rackets—which indeed are no great encumbrance, but a growing burden on a long march and on steep slopes most difficult to manage. We wore them for the rest of the day whenever we were walking on snow. About dawn the light became difficult; a thin floating mist confused the snow surfaces; ascents and descents were equally indistinguishable, so that the errant foot might unexpectedly hit the slope too soon or equally plunge down with sudden violence to unexpected depths. Crevasses forced, or seemed to force, us away to the right and over to the rocks of the left bank. We were faced with one of those critical decisions which determine success or failure. It seemed best to climb the rocks and avoid complications in the icefall. There was an easy way through on our left which we afterwards used; but perhaps we did well; ours was a certain way though long, and we had enough trudging that day; the rocks, though covered with snow to a depth of several inches, were not difficult, and a long traverse brought us back to the glacier at about 8.30 a.m.

Our greatest enemy as we went on was not, after all, the deep powdery snow. The racket sank slightly below the surface and carried a little snow each step as one lifted it; the work was arduous for the first man. But at a slow pace it was possible to plod on without undue exhaustion. The heat was a different matter. In the glacier-furnace the thin mist became steam, it enveloped us with a clinging garment from which no escape was possible, and far from being protected by it from the sun's fierce heat, we seemed to be scorched all the more because of it. The atmosphere was enervating to the last degree; to halt even for a few minutes was to be almost over-whelmed by inertia, so difficult it seemed, once the machinery had stopped and lost momentum, to heave it into motion again. And yet we must go on in one direction or the other or else succumb to sheer lassitude and overpowering drowsiness. The final slopes, about 700 feet at a fairly steep angle, undoubtedly called for greater efforts than any hitherto required of us.

The importance of breathing hard and deeply had impressed itself upon us again and again. I had come to think of my own prac-tice as a very definite and conscious performance adopted to suit the occasion. The principles were always the same—to time the breathing regularly to fit the step, and to use not merely the upper part of the lungs, but the full capacity of the breathing apparatus, expanding and contracting not the chest only, but also the diaphragm, and this not occasionally but with every breath when-ever the body was required to work at high pressure. Probably no one who has not tried it would guess how difficult it is to acquire an unconscious habit of deep breathing. It was easy enough to set the machine going in the right fashion; it was another task to keep it running. The moment attention to their performance was relaxed, the lungs too would begin to relax their efforts, and often I woke from some day-dream with a feeling of undue fatigue, to find the cause of my lassitude only in the lungs' laziness. The best chance of keeping them up to their work, I found, was to impose a rhythm pri-marily upon the lungs and swing the legs in time with it.

The practice employed for walking uphill under normal condi-tions is exactly contrary, in that case the rhythm is consciously imposed on the legs and the rest of the body takes care of itself.

During the various expeditions of our reconnaissance I came to employ two distinct methods of working the legs with the lungs. As soon as conscious breathing was necessary it was my custom delib-erately to inhale on one step and exhale on the next. Later, at a high-er elevation, or when the expenditure of muscular energy became more exhausting, I would both inhale and exhale for each step, in either case timing the first movement of lifting the leg to synchronise with the beginning, so to speak, of the breathing-stroke. On this occasion as we pushed our way up towards Lhakpa La I adopted a variation of this second method, a third stage, pausing a minute or so for the most furious sort of breathing after a series of steps, forty or thirty or twenty, as the strength ebbed, in order to gain potential energy for the next spasm of lifting efforts. Never before had our lungs been tested quite so severely. It was well for us that these final slopes were no steeper. It was difficult and tiring enough as it was to prevent the rackets sliding, though without them we could not possibly have advanced in such snow. But happily the consequences of a slip were not likely to be serious. We were able to struggle on without regarding dangers, half dazed with the heat and the glare and with mere fatigue, occasionally encouraged by a glimpse of the skyline above us, a clean edge of snow where the angle set back to the pass, more often enveloped in the scorching mist which made with the snow a continuous whiteness, so that the smooth slopes, even so near as where the foot must be placed next, was usually indistinguishable. We had proceeded a considerable distance and I was satisfied with our progress, when the leader broke the monotony; he was seen to hesitate in the act of stepping up, to topple over and fall headlong downwards. This time he had guessed wrong; his foot had hit unexpectedly against the steepening slope. Somehow he had passed in extreme fatigue from the physical state of stable equilibrium; he had become such a man as you may 'knock down with a feather', and this little misadventure had upset his balance. Mere surprise gave him strength to stop his slide. He raised himself, disgusted, to his feet again and after sundry gruntings the party went on.

Some little way further up Major Morshead, who was walking last in the party, with one brief exclamation to tell us what he intended, quietly untied the rope and remained where he was in his steps, unable to go further.

At length we found ourselves on flatter ground; the pass was still invisible, how far ahead of us we could not guess. Unexpectedly we came upon the brink of a crevasse. We worked round it, vaguely wondering whether after all our pains we were to meet with many troubles of this sort. And then after a few more steps we were visibly on some edge of things; we had reached the col itself.

Some twenty minutes later, as we sat on the snow gazing most intently at all that lay about us, Bullock and I were surprised by a shout. A moment later Major Morshead rejoined us, to the great rejoicing of all three.

It was about 1.15 p.m. when the first two of us had reached Lhakpa La; the clouds, which had been earlier only a thin veil, rent occasionally to give us clear glimpses, had thickened perceptibly during the last hour, so that we had now no hope of a clear view. In a sense, despite our early start from a high camp, we were too late. Little was to be seen above our level. The slopes of Everest away on our left were visible only where they impinged upon the glacier. But we were not actually in cloud on the col. The South-facing rocks of Changtse presented their profile, steep and jagged, an imposing spectacle so far up as we could see; between them and Everest we looked down on a broad bay, the smooth surface of which was only occasionally broken by large crevasses. The descent to it from where we were could also be seen well enough, and we judged it perfectly simple and not much more than 800 feet.[12] The East ridge of Changtse had no existence for us; we looked across at what presumably were the splayed-out slopes supporting it. Below them was a narrow glacier (it grew when we crossed it to broader dimensions), shaping its course somewhat to the West of North, joined after losing its white snow-covering by another and cleaner glacier coming steeply down from the left, then apparently bending with this confluent to the right, and finally lost to view. We could see no more; the mountain sides, which must hem it in on the

North, remained completely hidden, and for all we had seen the exit of this glacier was still a mystery.

Another great question remained unsolved. We had been able to make out the way across the head of the glacier towards the wall under Chang La; and the way was easy enough. But the wall itself, in spite of some fleeting glimpses and partial revelations, we had never really seen. We conjectured its height should be 500 feet or little more; and it was probably steep. It had been impossible to found an opinion as to whether the col were accessible. Nevertheless, I held an opinion, however flimsy the foundations. I had seen the rim of the col from both sides, and knew that above it on either hand were unserrated edges. When we added to whatever chances might be offered by the whole extent of the wall, which was considerable, the possibilities of finding a way to the col by the slopes of Everest

South-East Ridge of Mount Everest from above the 20,000 foot camp, Kharta Valley.

to the South or by those of Changtse to the North, I felt we had enough in our favour. I was prepared, so to speak, to bet my bottom dollar that a way could be found, and was resolved that before we turned homewards this year we must get up from the East. When I thought of the 4,000 feet on the other side, the length combined with the difficulties, the distance that would necessarily separate us there from any convenient base and all the limitations in our strength, I could have no reasonable doubt that here to the East lay the best chance of success.

It remained to determine by which of two possible routes we should reach the glacier-head between Lhakpa La and Chang La. Presuming that Wheeler was right, we could use the old base at the foot of the Rongbuk Glacier which was only one stage, though a very long one, from Chöbu, and proceed simply enough by two rough marches and one which should be easier to a camp at the foot of the wall or possibly to the col itself. On the East we could use as an advanced base a place two easy marches from Kharta; from there I reckoned one long day and two easy ones, provided the snow were hard, to Chang La. Against this route was the loss of height in crossing Lhakpa La; and for it the convenience of a good encampment on stones at 20,000 feet, better than anything we might expect to find at a similar elevation on the other side. So far the pros and cons were evenly balanced. But there was one great and perhaps insuperable obstacle in working from the Rongbuk Valley. We had always found difficulties there in obtaining an adequate supply of fuel. There is no wood at Chöbu or for some distance below it. A few small bushes grow in a little patch of vegetation by the riverside an hour higher up. But it is a very niggardly supply, and when I thought of the larger scale of the preparations we should now have to make, it became clear that we should have to rely on gobar, which, besides being a more extravagant fuel in the sense that it gives less fire for a given weight than wood, is also difficult to get in the Rongbuk Valley, for little enough is to be found there, and the monastery at Chöyling is a large consumer. On the other hand, in the Kharta Valley we were in a land of plenty. Gobar and rhododendron were to be had within a stone's throw of our present Advanced Base Camp, and a little lower was an abundance of juniper. Food supplies also were better here; fresh vegetables and eggs, luxuries never seen on the other side, could easily be obtained from Kharta, and even the sheep in this region could be praised at the expense of the Rongbuk breed, which was incomparably skinny; lurking in the thigh of one recently killed we had actually discovered a nugget of fat.

And presuming Wheeler were wrong? In any case we knew enough of the country to be sure that a valley further to the North would offer us little better than the Rongbuk Valley, for it must be situated in the drier area unvisited by the monsoon currents from the Arun. The conclusion was drawn as we came down from Lhakpa La more swiftly than the reader of these arguments might suppose. We had now found a way to approach Chang La—not an ideal way, because it would involve a descent, and not one that could be used immediately; but good enough for our purpose.[13] About the beginning of the month the monsoon would come to an end; then we should have a succession of bright, clear days to melt the snow and cold, starry nights to freeze it hard.

The abiding thought, therefore, after the first rush downwards on the steep slopes below the col contained a measure of solid satisfaction. We had now brought to an end our preliminary reconnaissance. Ahead of us was a new phase in our operations, and one which should hold in store for us the finest adventure of all, the climax of all reconnoitring expeditions, that advance which was to bring us as near to the summit as our strength would take us. As we plodded on, retracing our steps, some little satisfaction was highly acceptable. To the tired party even descent seemed laborious. We reached the edge of the glacier where we had come on to it at 5.30 p.m. But the march from there to our lower camp was both long and rough. Major Morshead, who had not been trained with Bullock and me to the pace of such expeditions, had kept up to far in the gamest fashion; but he was now much exhausted. The day ended with a series of little spur., balancing over the snow-sprinkled boulders along and along the valley, in the dim misty moonlit scene, until at 2 o'clock in the morning we reached our lower camp, twenty-three hours after the early start.

On 20 August we went down to Kharta for ten days' rest and reorganisation. The party was gathering there for the assault, in which all were to help to the best of their powers. Col. Howard-Bury and Mr Wollaston were there; Dr. Heron came in on the following day, and a little later Major Wheeler. A conversation with this officer, who had been working in the Rongbuk Valley since Bullock and I had left it, was naturally of the highest interest, and he now confirmed what his sketch-map had suggested: that the glacier on to which we had looked down from Lhakpa La drained into the Rongbuk Valley. But this certain knowledge could have no bearing on our plans; we remained content with the way we had found and troubled our heads no more for the present about the East Rongbuk Glacier.

6d
The Assault

In the agreeable climate of Kharta we were sufficiently occupied with the results of photography and preparations for the future; and there was time besides for unmixed idleness, which we knew how to appreciate. Our thoughts turned often to the weather. Local lore confirmed our expectations for September, and we looked each day for signs of a change. It was arranged, in hope if not in confidence, to move up on the first signs of improvement. Already before we came down to Kharta our Advanced Base Camp had been moved up; it was now situated at about 17,300 feet on a convenient grassy plateau and only a reasonable stage below our 20,000-foot camp, where some light tents and stores had also been left. At these two camps we had, in fact, left everything which we should not absolutely require at Kharta, so that few mountaineering stores would have to be carried forward from the Base when we came up again. Our first task would be to supply the Advanced Base with food and fuel, and a start had already been made by collecting here a pile of wood, nominally thirty loads. Transport in any case was not likely to be a difficulty in the early stages. Local coolies could easily be hired, and Howard-Bury was to follow us up after a short interval with all available strength to help in every possible way.[14]

It was comparatively a simple matter to provide the earlier camps. The first above the Advanced Base—that at 20,000 feet— could be filled before we moved up to sleep there, the coolies returning on the same day whenever they carried up loads. And the same plan could be adopted for the second at Lhakpa La; only one journey there, I calculated, would be required before we started in force from the 20,000-foot camp to go straight ahead without delay. The crux would lie in the stage from Lhakpa La to Chang La. At the most we should have twenty-three coolies, sixteen who had been all along with the climbing party, three whom Wheeler had partially trained, and four more Sherpas, the maximum number being determined by the supply of boots. But it would not be necessary to carry on all the loads from Lhakpa La; and return journeys could be made from Chang La both by those who were not to stay there and by twelve already mentioned who might fetch supplies if necessary on the final day of the assault. This plan was never executed in its later stages, and we cannot know for certain whether it would have held good. But it may be conjectured, in view of our experience, that the weakest link would have broken; either an extra day would have been spent between Lhakpa La and Chang La, or, if we had reached Chang La according to our programme with the minimum of supplies, the coolies would not have been brought to this point a second time and the climbing party would have been cut off from its reserves. And, granted the most favourable conditions for the attempt, in asking the coolies to carry loads of 30 lb. on two consecutive days at these high altitudes, we were probably expecting too much of them. It must be concluded, if this opinion is correct, that we had not enough coolies for what we intended.

On the last day of August, Bullock and I were established once again at our Advanced Base. The weather had not yet cleared, though it was showing some signs of change. But it had been necessary to move up for the coolies' sake. At Kharta, where they found little to amuse them and no work to employ their time, they had sought diversion with the aid of liquor and became discontented and ill-affected. They were badly in need of a routine, which at the Advanced Base was easily enough provided. Besides, I wanted to be ready, and it seemed not too soon to begin carrying loads up to the next camp. There was no occasion for hurry in the event. We were obliged to wait nearly three weeks, until 19 September, before moving forward. The delay served no useful purpose, the work of supplying our present needs and providing for the future was sufficiently spread over the long tale of days, but interspersed with more rest and leisure than anyone required.

In some respects life at the Advanced Base compared favourably with our experience at other camps. The place had a charm of its own. The short turf about us, the boulders and little streams reminded me of Welsh hillsides; and these high pastures were often decorated by the brilliant blues of Gentiana Ornata and by the most exquisite of saxifrages, which, with the yellow and ochre markings on the cream glaze of its tiny bowl, recalls the marginal ornament on some Persian page. Whenever the weather cleared for a few hours we saw down the valley a splendid peak in a scene of romantic beauty, and by walking up to a stony shoulder only 2,000 feet above us, we had amazing views of Everest and Makalu. And it was an advantage during these days of waiting to be a larger party, as we soon became.

Bury and Wollaston, and also Raeburn whom we rejoiced to see again, had come up on the 6th, Morshead and Wheeler on the 11th, and for two nights Heron was of our company. We made little excursions to keep ourselves fit, and on one occasion enjoyed some rock-climbing. But it amused nobody to watch the procession of clouds which precipitated sleet by day and snow by night, and our appetite for adventure could not be stimulated by making time pass in some endurable fashion and counting the unhopeful signs.

Under these circumstances I became more than ever observant

of the party's physical condition. I find a passage in one of my letters written during this period of waiting in which I boast of finding myself 'still able to go up about 1,500 feet in an hour not bad going at these altitudes'—a reassuring statement enough but for the one word 'still', which betrays all my anxiety. In fact there was too much cause to be anxious. Three of our strongest coolies were ill at this camp; others seemed to be tired more easily than they should be. And what of the Sahibs? At least it must be said that several of them were not looking their best. Bullock, though he never complained, seemed no longer to be the fit man he was at the end of July. And for my part I began to experience a certain lack of exuberance when going up hill. I came to realise that all such efforts were unduly exhausting; my reserve of strength had somehow diminished. The whole machine, in fact, was running down; the days continued to pass with their cloud and rain and snow, always postponing our final effort to a later date and a colder season; and with them our chances of success were slowly vanishing.

When at last the weather cleared, it was evident that the fate of our enterprise would be decided by the sun's power to melt the snow. In a subsequent chapter I shall have more to say about the snow's melting; it may suffice to remark here that, before we left the Advanced Base, I had good reason to expect that we should meet adverse conditions, and was resolved at the same time that nothing was to be gained by waiting. The coolies were tightly laden up to the First Advanced Camp and sufficiently unfatigued to proceed next day. On the 20th, therefore, leaving Bullock to accompany Wheeler, Morshead and I set forth to get fourteen loads up to Lhakpa La, We had one spare coolie who carried no load, and Sanglu, who was now our acting Sirdar, four of us in all, to break the trail for the loaded men. Snow-shoes were not carried because there were not enough to go round. Though our prospects of reaching a high point on Everest were already sufficiently dim, I intended to carry out the original plan until obliged by circumstances to modify it; it might prove necessary to spend an extra day in reaching Chang La, and in that case we could perhaps afford to stop short of Lhakpa La and establish our camp below its final slopes. But if the strain on this first day was likely to be severe, I argued that the coolies could rest tomorrow, and that the second journey in frozen tracks would be easy enough. That we should be passing the night a few hundred feet higher (at 22,500 feet) was a relatively unimportant consideration. The great matter was to put heart into the coolies; it would be infinitely more encouraging to reach the crest with a sense of complete achievement, to see the clear prospect ahead and to proceed downwards on the other side.

Our start at an early hour on the 20th was propitious enough. It was the same moonlit glacier of our expedition a month before as we made good our approach to its surface. But the conditions were altered. For the first time since we had come to these mountains we experienced the wonderful delight of treading snow that is both crisp and solid. We walked briskly over it, directly towards Mount Everest, with all the hope such a performance might inspire. The night was exceedingly cold and there was no untoward delay. In less than an hour we were at the foot of the icefall. We were determined on this occasion not to avoid it by the rocks of the left bank, but to find a quicker way through the tumbled ice. At first all went well. A smooth-floored corridor took us helpfully upwards. And then, in the dim light, we were among the crevasses. To be seriously held up here might well be fatal to our object, and in the most exciting kind of mountaineering adventures we had the stimulus of this thought. We plunged into the maze and struggled for a little time, crossing frail bridges over fantastic depths and making steps up steep little walls, until it seemed we were in serious trouble. One leap proposed by the leader proved too much for some of the laden coolies and a good deal of pushing and pulling was required to bring them over the formidable gap. We had begun to waste time. Halted on a sharp little crest between two monstrous chasms Morshead and I discussed the situation, and thereafter gravely proceeded to reconnoitre the ground to our left. In ten minutes we came to another corridor like the first, which brought us out above the icefall.

We were well satisfied with our progress as we halted at sunrise, and it was a pleasant change to get our feet out of the snow and knock a little warmth into chilled toes. But our confidence had ebbed. Even as we entered the icefall our feet had occasionally broken the crust; as we came out of it we were stamping a trail.

Dorji Gompa, our unladen coolie, and perhaps the strongest man of all, took the lead when we went on, and plugged manfully upwards. But already the party was showing signs of fatigue. One coolie, and then two others, fell out and could not be induced to come further. I sent Dorji Gompa back to bring on one of their loads. Morshead, Sanglu and I took turns ahead and soon came to the worst snow we had encountered anywhere. In it no firm steps could be stamped by the leaders to save the coolies behind, and each man in turn had to contend with the shifting substance of fine powder. The party straggled badly. It was necessary for some of us to press on and prove that the goal could be reached. Many of the men were obliged to halt at frequent intervals. But time was on our side. Gradually the party fought its way up the final slopes. As we approached the pass I looked back with Morshead over the little groups along our track and saw some distance below the last moving figure another lying huddled up on the snow. I soon learnt the meaning of this: it was Dorji Gompa who lay there. He had carried on not one load as I had asked him, but two, until he had fallen there dazed and exhausted.

At length eleven loads reached the pass and two more were only 800 feet lower. If we had not done all we set out to do I was satisfied we had done enough. We had established tracks to Lhakpa La which would serve us well when they had frozen hard, and not too many loads remained below to be brought up two days later.

We now obtained a clear view of Chang La; it was possible to make more exact calculations, and it was evident we must modify our plans. We saw a wall of formidable dimensions, perhaps 1,000 feet high; the surface was unpleasantly broken by insuperable bergschrunds and the general angle was undoubtedly steep. The slopes of Everest to the South were out of the question, and if it were possible to avoid a direct assault by the North side the way here would be long, difficult and exceedingly laborious. The wall itself offered the best chance, and I was in good hopes we could get up. But it would not be work for untrained men, and to have on the rope a number of laden coolies, more or less mountain-sick, conducted by so small a nucleus as three Sahibs, who would also presumably be feeling the effects of altitude, was a proposition not to be contemplated for a moment. We must have as strong a party as possible in the first place, simply to reach the col, and afterwards to bring up a camp, if we were able, as a separate operation. With this idea I selected the party. Wollaston felt that his place of duty was not with the van; only Wheeler besides had sufficient mountaineering experience, and it was decided that he alone should accompany Bullock and myself on our first attempt to reach the col. Nevertheless, it seemed undesirable to abandon so early the hope that Bury and Morshead would be of use to us later on; and Wollaston clearly must start with us from the 20,000-foot camp where all had gathered on the 20th.[15]

On the col beyond it was blowing a gale. And higher was a more fearful sight. The powdery fresh snow on the great face of Everest was being swept along in unbroken spindrift and the very ridge where our route lay was marked out to receive its unmitigated fury. We could see the blown snow deflected upwards for a moment where the wind met the ridge, only to rush violently down in a frightful blizzard on the leeward side. To see, in fact, was enough; the wind had settled the question; it would have been folly to go on. Nevertheless, some little discussion took place as to what might be possible, and we struggled a few steps further to put the matter to the test. For a few moments we exposed ourselves on the col to feel the full strength of the blast, then struggled back to shelter. Nothing more was said about pushing our assault any further.[16]

Without consulting the meteorologist at Simla it is difficult to accept assertions about the monsoon as ultimate truth. Beyond a general, rather vague, agreement as to what should normally be expected, opinions differ not a little as to the measure and frequency of divergences from the norm. And individuals who observe in one locality more or less than they hope or expect are apt to forget that their dearth or plenty may be elsewhere compensated by capricious incidence. Nevertheless it seems certain that this year's rainfall in North-east India was above the normal both in amount and duration. 'We had good rain,' people said, and I was tempted to reply, 'We had bad snow.' Travelling through India I frequently asked questions on this point, and almost invariably heard of an unusually bountiful rainfall, seldom of one which was merely sufficient. Inhabitants of Darjeeling, who have observed the hills in the changing seasons for many years, told me that it was almost unheard of that so much snow should fall in September and lie so low. The general tenor of such remarks may probably be applied to an area including not only Mount Everest itself and the great peaks in its neighbourhood, but also a considerable tract of country to the North. The monsoon, according to Tibetan information, started perhaps a little later than usual, but was still more late in coming to an end; the Tibetans ordinarily lie with an object, and there could be no object in deceiving us about the weather. It may be concluded the year was abnormally wet, though to what extent on Everest itself can hardly be divined.

During our outward journey through Sikkim we saw nothing of the high peaks. The weather was not necessarily bad because the peaks were veiled. When we first saw Everest from Khamba Dzong on 6 June, it was obscured some three hours after sunrise, but the weather seemed fine: and on two subsequent days we made the same observation. On 13 June, from the hills above Shiling, Bullock and I were trying to make out the Everest group through glasses for about three hours. When first we looked in that direction, it appeared that a storm was in progress, with dark clouds drifting up from the West; but Kanchenjunga at the same time was a glorious sight, and all the mountains were clear before sunset. The most splendid of the distant views was from Ponglet on 19 June: we were up our hill half an hour after sunrise and half an hour later there was nothing to be seen. There may have been malice in the clouds that day. It was radiantly fine where we were; but in the afternoon we came under the edge of a storm which drenched the main body of the Expedition as they were approaching Tingri; and there was a definite break in the weather at this time.

I suppose this break may be taken as the forerunner of the monsoon on Mount Everest. Storms there may have been before; but, generally speaking, it had been fine over the mountains since the beginning of June, and though the evidence is slight enough it seems probable that Everest received little or no snow before 20 June. When first we saw it, a few days later, from the Rongbuk Glacier, it was still comparatively black. It appeared a rocky mass with a white arm to the right, some permanent snow on the ledges and in the gullies of the face turned Northwards in our direction and some snow again on the high North-east arête; but with no pretensions to be a snow-mountain, a real sugar-cake as it seemed afterwards to become. We were lucky in having a few fine days at the outset of our reconnaissance. The conditions then were very different from those which obtained later. The recent snow must have melted quickly; we found clean ice on an East-facing slope at 21,000 feet and also at a gentler angle on one facing West. On Ri-ring the slopes were generally covered with snow near the crest, thinly but sufficiently, or we should never have got up; near the summit we found ice on both sides, North and South. It is impossible to say up to what height one might have found ice in June. Appearances suggested that on all but the steepest slopes above 23,000 feet the surface was hard snow rather than ice.

It was on the day following our ascent of Ri-ring, 6 July, that we first experienced a real snowfall; and we woke next morning to find three or four inches covering the ground. In so far as an exact date can be ascribed to what is hardly a single event, 6-7 July may be taken as the beginning of the monsoon. We imagined at first that this snowfall was an important matter, sufficient to prevent climbing at any considerable height for several days. But from subsequent observations we came to treat such snowfalls with a certain degree of contempt. It was more often than not the case during the whole of July until the date of our departure that snow fell during the day—sometimes perhaps for a comparatively short period between noon and sunset, not seldom for many hours, intermittently during the day from the middle of the morning, and continuing into the night. But it was often so far as we were concerned a harmless phenomenon. Snow was precipitated from clouds so thin that they were easily penetrated by the sun's heat; it melted where it lay, and the moisture so readily evaporated that the snow had hardly stopped falling before the ground was dry. One might suppose that a few hundred feet higher, where the snow could be seen to lie where it fell, the effects would be more severe; but it was remarkable after half a day's unceasing precipitation of this fine granular snow that one might go up early next morning, perhaps to 20,000 feet, and find no more than a thin covering of 2 or 3 inches on the stones.

In saying that this sort of weather was harmless, I am not denying that it hindered our operations; but from the point of view merely of the climber it was remarkably innocuous. A more disagreeable experience was our first journey to the col from which we afterwards looked into the West cwm of Everest; we reached the pass in the teeth of a wind which drove the snow into our faces; but the weather had no real sting, and the wind, though cold, seemed to touch us lightly. Wind, in fact, was never an enemy to be feared during the whole period of the monsoon, and snowstorms, though they prevented more than one expedition, never turned us back. The delays in our reconnaissance caused by bad weather were of course considerable; we were forced to push our camps higher than would have otherwise been necessary, and often found ourselves hurrying after a start before dawn in a desperate race with the clouds to reach a view-point before the view had disappeared. And the precipitation of snow on the glaciers forced us invariably to wear snow-shoes on nevé, and consequently limited the numbers in our parties.

I have already alluded to a more serious snowfall which took place from 20 to 25 July. Another occurred during the first days of August and another again on 20 and 21 August, when snow came down below 15,000 feet. In September, towards the end of the monsoon, the weather was more monotonously malicious and the snowfall tended to be heavier; I find two heavy falls noted particularly in my diary. But on the whole it was the habit of snow to fall lightly. It is remarkable, when one calls to mind such a big snowfall as may occur during the climbing season in the Alps before the weather is resolved to be fine, how little snow by comparison fell on any one day in the region of Mount Everest. And perhaps in the end the slopes were more laden by the smaller precipitations which deposited a daily accretion.

We naturally sought an answer to the interminable query as to how much melting took place at the highest altitudes. Melting of course was always quicker on rocks. But even on the glaciers it was remarkably rapid whenever the sun shone brightly, and we were more than once surprised after a period of cloudy weather with constant snow showers to find how much the snow had consolidated. It seemed to us on more than one occasion that while snow had been falling at our camps and on the lower peaks, Everest itself must have escaped. But, generally speaking, after 6 July the mountain was remarkably white and became increasingly whiter, and only at the least two perfectly fine days, which rarely came together, made any perceptible difference. It was remarkable how little ice was ever observable on the steep Eastern face, where one would expect to see icicles hanging about the rocks. It is my own impression for what it is worth, and its value I fear is small, that though snow will melt readily enough low down, at least up to 23,000 feet during the warmer weather even on cloudy days, at greater altitudes, perhaps above 25,000 feet, it rarely melts even in bright sunshine. In September this year I doubt if it melted at all above 23,000 feet after the weather cleared. At lower elevations direction and angle of the slope made all the difference. After one fine day the snow on a steep East slope had solidified to a remarkable degree at about 20,000 feet; on a North-facing slope at a similar elevation it had been quite unaffected; on flat surfaces 1,000 feet higher a perceptible crust had formed, but the snow remained powdery below it as on the day when it fell. After three or four fine days the snowy surface of a glacier was absolutely hard at about 20,000 feet and remained solid in the afternoon. Fifteen hundred feet higher we were breaking a hard crust and sinking in a foot or more. This condition may have been partly due to the local behaviour of clouds, which were apt to cling about a ridge overlooking the glacier and cast a shadow on this part of it. But higher, on more open ground, we met the same condition; and again the slopes facing North preserved a powdery snow which never changed before it was blown down in avalanches. Perhaps the most convincing phenomena were the powdery snow high up on the Eastern slopes under the North Col and the snow on the Western slopes at a similar elevation under Lhakpa La, which was hardly more solid, while 1,000 feet lower we found excellent snow. It is difficult to resist the conclusion that altitude is a determining factor in the sun's power of melting. It is possible that a line might always be drawn on any given day above which the temperature of the air is too cold for snow to melt where it has fallen on snow, and another to meet the case where it covers rocks. From our all too limited observations in June I should judge that in the middle of summer such imaginary lines would be above the height of Everest, but in other and cooler seasons we should quickly find them lower and a long way below the summit.

In close connection with the snow's melting we had to consider the possibility of avalanches. Our observations on this head were so meagre that I can only make with the greatest diffidence a few statements about them. It is astonishing to reflect how seldom we either saw or heard an avalanche, or even noticed the débris of one under steep slopes which had been laden with snow. Only on two occasions, I believe, were we confronted in practice with the question as to whether a slope could safely be crossed. The first was on 7 August in ascending the peak Carpo-ri, of which I have previously made mention. The heavy snowfall at the beginning of the month had ceased during the night 4-5 August; the following days had been warm but cloudy, and on both there had been prolonged snow showers of the lighter sort in the afternoon and evening. On the night of 6 August we had hard frost at 17,500 feet, and there was to considerable sprinkling of fresh snow on the stones of the moraine. Between the col and the summit we met some very steep snow slopes on the South side: we carried no clinometer and I shall not venture to estimate their angles of inclination. It was on this occasion, as I have narrated, that in crossing a shallow scoop I was very much afraid of an avalanche, but was able to choose a safe line where we were protected and helped by an island of rocks. The snow here was inclined to be powdery; but it had solidified in some degree and, where we had to tread it, adhered sufficiently to the slope so as to give one a distinct confidence that it would not slide off wherever it might be crossed. Above this place we were able to avoid danger by following an edge where the snow was not so deep; but here again I noticed with surprise the adhesion between new snow and old. The ice below was not solid and smooth, but frothy and rough, and easily penetrated by a strong blow of the axe; it seemed to have been formed very quickly. The snow showed no inclination to slide off, though it was not of the substance in which a secure step could be made: and I concluded that the process of assimilation between the old surface and the new snow must proceed very rapidly whenever the temperature was warm enough. On the final slope, which was even steeper, more snow was lying—it was a more powdery substance: I was able again to escape danger on an edge dividing two faces; but it was surprising that no avalanche had already taken place and that the snow contrived to stay where it was.

The other was in traversing the slopes to the North Col. Here our feet undoubtedly found a solid bed to tread upon, but the substance above it was dubiously loose. It was my conviction at the time that with axes well driven in above us we were perfectly safe here. But on the way down we observed a space of five yards or so where the surface snow had slid away below our tracks. The disquieting thoughts that necessarily followed this discovery left and still leave me in some doubt as to how great a risk, if any, we were actually taking. But it is natural to suppose that at a higher elevation or in a cooler season, because the snow adheres less rapidly to the slopes on which it lies, an avalanche of new snow is more likely to occur.

Temperature

Before attempting to draw conclusions as to the relative chances of finding favourable conditions between one month and another, a few words must be said about temperature.

So far as the temperature of the air was concerned, we experienced no severe cold and suffered no hardships from first to last. I do not mean to affirm that it was always warm. We welcomed frost at nights as one does in the Alps. In general it may be said that there could be no difficulty in providing equipment against any cold we encountered. Heat was a much more dangerous enemy, as I indicated in describing our first ascent to Lhakpa La. Personally I never felt the sun's power on my head, but I felt it on my back so early as 8 a.m. as a definite attack on my energy and vital power, and more than once, though the sun was not shining, in crossing a glacier late in the day I was reduced from a state of alert activity to one of heavy lassitude.

The temperature of the snow is another consideration of very great importance. Even in July I felt the snow to be cold in the middle of the day towards the summit of Ri-ring, and when wearing snow-shoes in fresh snow under 20,000 feet coolies and all felt the cold in their feet. Later I apprehended a real danger from this source. The coolies were encouraged to anoint their feet with whale oil, and we avoided accident and even complaint: but I always admired their resistance to cold. Personally, though I am not particularly a cold-footed person, I took the precaution of wearing two pairs of long socks which were both new and thick, and a third from which, unfortunately, the toes had to be amputated owing to the timid miscalculation of my bootmaker: this equipment sufficed and I found my feet perfectly warm, while one of my companions was obliged to pull off a boot in order to restore circulation, and the other went on with numb feet and barely escaped frost-bite. And I must again emphasise the fact that this was on an Eastern slope well warmed by the sun in the middle of the morning and at an altitude no higher than about 22,500 feet. It may readily be concluded that forethought and care are in no respect more necessary than in guarding against frozen feet among a large party at the highest altitudes. And the difficulty of guarding against this danger might well determine the limits at either end of the warmest weather within which an assault should be launched on Everest itself or any of the half-dozen or so highest peaks.

The best season for climbing

It will hardly be doubtful from the whole tendency of my preceding remarks about weather and conditions that my opinion inclines decisively to the earlier rather than the later season as offering the best chances of climbing Mount Everest. We cannot of course assume that because September was a bad month this year it will always be a bad month. But supposing the monsoon were to end punctually and a fair spell to have set in by the first day of September—even then it appears to me improbable that the fresh snow fallen during the monsoon would sufficiently melt near the top of the mountain two and a half months after midsummer. As to the prospects of wind, we can only be content with the statement that in this particular year the wind after the end of the monsoon would alone have defeated even the most determined attempt to reach the summit. A wind strong enough to blow up the snow must always, I believe, prevent an ascent. A superman might perhaps be found, but never a party of men whose endurance at high altitudes would warrant the risk of exhaustion in struggling for long hours against such adverse circumstances. For the earlier season it may be said again, as a simple observation upon which little enough can be built, that the appearance of the clouds before the monsoon did not suggest wind, but rather a calm air on the summit. What precisely the conditions may be, for instance, in May and June, 1922, or what we ought normally to expect, cannot be determined with certainty.

Will the whole of the snow fallen during the monsoon of 1921 have melted before the next monsoon, and if so by what date? Will the amount of snow on the mountain be the same in June, 1922, as twelve months before? Or will black and white appear in altered proportions? And if the snow has melted, where will ice be found? It might well be that under the North Col all the steeper slopes will have lost their snow. And what of the final arête? One conjecture seems as good as another, and the experience of more travelled mountaineers will suggest the most probable answer to these questions with an instinct less fallible than mine. Nevertheless, I think it may be said that the chances are all in favour of the earlier season. One must prefer the lesser of two evils. Ice is far from an insuperable obstacle on Mount Everest; almost anywhere above Chang La crampons would overcome it: but powdery snow, in case the snow has melted too little, is a deadly handicap. Finally, the earlier is the warmer season with less danger to vulnerable feet and requiring a lighter equipment.

6f
The Route to the Summit

The reader who has carefully followed the preceding story will hardly have failed to notice that the route which has been chosen as the only one offering reasonable chances of success remains still very largely a matter of speculation. But the reconnaissance, unless it were actually to reach the summit, was obliged to leave much unproved, and its value must depend upon observations in various sorts and not merely upon the practice of treading the snow and rocks. Speculation in this case is founded upon experience of certain phenomena and a study of the mountain's features; and it is by relating what has been only seen with known facts that inferences have been drawn.

It may perhaps be accounted a misfortune that the party of 1921 did not approach Chang La by the East Rongbuk Glacier. The Lhakpa La proved a bigger obstacle than was expected. But in conditions such as we hope to find before the monsoon, this way would have much to recommend it. It avoids all laborious walking on a dry glacier, and with hard snow the walk up to the pass from the camp on stones at 20,000 feet should not be unduly fatiguing. Still the fact remains that the descent from the Lhakpa La on to the East Rongbuk Glacier is not less than 1,200 feet. Would it not be better to follow up this glacier from the Rongbuk Valley? The absence of wood on this side need not deter the party of 1922. For them plenty of time will be available sufficiently to provide their base with fuel, and the sole consideration should be the easiest line of approach; and though no one has traversed the whole length of the East Rongbuk Glacier, enough is known to choose this way with confidence. Here, as on other glaciers which we saw, the difficulties clearly lie below the limit of perpetual snow, and the greater part of them were avoided or solved by Major Wheeler, who found a practicable way on to the middle of the glacier at about 19,000 feet, and felt certain that the medial moraine ahead of him would serve for an ascent and be no more arduous than the moraines of the West Rongbuk Glacier had proved to be. The view of this way from the Lhakpa La confirmed his opinion, and though it may be called a speculation to choose it, whereas the way from the East has been established by experiment, it is a fair inference from experience to conclude that the untraversed section of the East Rongbuk Glacier, a distance which could be accomplished very easily in one march if all went well, will afford a simple approach to Chang La.

The Eastern wall, about 1,000 feet high, by which the gap itself must be reached, can never be lightly esteemed. Here reconnaissance has forged a link. But those who reached the col were not laden with tents and stores; and on another occasion the conditions may be different. There may be the danger of an avalanche or the difficulty of ice. From what we saw this year before the monsoon had brought a heavy snowfall it is by no means improbable that ice will be found at the end of May on the steepest slope below Chang La. In that case much labour will be required to hew and keep in repair a staircase, and perhaps fix a banister, so that the laden coolies, not all of whom will be competent ice-men, may be brought up in safety.

The summit of Mount Everest is about 6,000 feet above Chang La; the distance is something like 2½ miles and the whole of it is unexplored. What grounds have we for thinking that the mountaineering difficulties will not prove insuperable, that in so far as mere climbing is concerned the route is practicable? Two factors, generally speaking, have to be considered: the nature of the ground and the general angle of inclination. Where the climber is confined to a narrow crest and can find no way to circumvent an obstacle, a very small tower or wall, a matter of twenty feet, may bar his progress. There the general angle may be what it likes: the important matter for him is that the angle is too steep in a particular place. But on a mountain's face where his choice is not limited to a strict and narrow way, the general angle is of primary importance: if it is sufficiently gentle, the climber will find that he may wander almost where he will to avoid the steeper places. Long before we reached Chang La Mr Bullock and I were fairly well convinced that the slope from here to the North-east Shoulder was sufficiently gentle and that the nature of the ill-defined ridge connecting these two points was not such as to limit the choice of route to a narrow line. Looking up from the North Col, we learnt nothing more about the angles. The view, however, was not without value; it amply confirmed our opinion as to the character of what lay ahead of us. The ridge is not a crest; its section is a wide and rounded angle. It is not decorated by pinnacles, it does not rise in steps. It presents a smooth continuous way, and whether the rocks are still covered with powdery snow, or only slightly sprinkled and for the most part bare, the party of 1922 should be able to go up a long way at all events without meeting any serious obstacle. It may not prove a perfectly simple matter actually to reach the North-east arête above the shoulder at about 28,000 feet. The angle becomes steeper towards this arête. But even in the last section below it, the choice of a way should not be inconveniently restricted. On the right of the ascending party will be permanent snow on various sloping ledges, an easy alternative to rocks if the snow is found in good condition, and always offering a detour by which to avoid an obstacle.

From the North-east Shoulder to the summit of the mountain the way is not so smooth. The rise is only 1,000 feet in a distance of half a mile, but the first part of the crest is distinctly jagged by several towers and the last part is steep. Much will depend upon the possibility of escaping from the crest to avoid the obstacles and of regaining it easily. The South-east side (left going up) is terribly steep, and it will almost certainly be out of the question to traverse there. But the sloping snow-covered ledges on the North-west may serve very well; the difficulty about them is their tendency to be horizontal in direction and to diverge from the arête where it slopes upwards, so that a party which had followed one in preference to the crest might find themselves cut off by a cliff running across the face above them. But one way or another I think it should be possible with the help of such ledges to reach the final obstacle. The summit itself is like the thin end of a wedge thrust up from the mass in which it is embedded. The edge of it, with the highest point at the far end, can only be reached from the North-east by climbing a steep blunt edge of snow. The height of this final obstacle must be fully 200 feet. Mr Bullock and I examined it often through our field-glasses, and though it did not appear insuperable, whatever our point of view, it never looked anything but steep.

To determine whether it is humanly possible to climb to the summit of Mount Everest or what may be the chances of success in such an undertaking, other factors besides the mere mountaineering difficulties have to be considered. It is at least probable that the obstacles presented by this mountain could be overcome by any competent party if they met them in the Alps. But it is a very different matter to be confronted with such obstacles at elevations between 23,000 and 29,000 feet. We do not know that it is physiologically possible at such high altitudes for the human body to make the efforts required to lift itself up even on the simplest ground. The condition of the party of 1921 in September during the days of the Assault cannot be taken as evidence that the feat is impossible. The long periods spent in high camps and the tax of many exhausting expeditions had undoubtedly reduced the physical efficiency of Sahibs and coolies alike. The party of 1922, on the other hand, will presumably choose for their attempt a time when the climbers are at the top of their form and their powers will depend on the extent of their adaptability to the condition of high altitude. Nothing perhaps was so astonishing in the party of reconnaissance as the rapidity with which they became acclimatised and capable of great exertions between 18,000 and 21,000 feet. Where is the limit of this process? Will the multiplication of red corpuscles continue so that men may become acclimatised much higher? There is evidence enough to show that they may exist comfortably enough, eating and digesting hearty meals and retaining a feeling of vitality and energy up to 23,000 feet. It may be that, after two or three days quietly spent at this height, the body would sufficiently adjust itself to endure the still greater difference from normal atmospheric pressure 6,000 feet higher. At all events, a practical test can alone provide the proof in such a case. Experiments carried out in a laboratory by putting a man into a sealed chamber and reducing the pressure say to half an atmosphere, valuable as they may be when related to the experiences of airmen, can establish nothing for mountaineers; for they leave out of account the all-important physiological factor of acclimatisation. But in any case it is to be expected that efforts above 23,000 feet will be more exhausting than those at lower elevations; and it may well be that the nature of the ground will turn the scale against the climber. For him it is all important that he should be able to breathe regularly, the demand upon his lungs along the final arête cannot fail to be a terrible strain, and anything like a tussle up some steep obstacle which would interfere with the regularity of his breathing might prove to be an ordeal beyond his strength.

As a way out of these difficulties of breathing, the use of oxygen has often been recommended and experiments were made by Dr. Kellas,[17] which will be continued in 1922.

Even so there will remain the difficulty of establishing one or perhaps two camps above Chang La (23,000 feet). It is by no means certain that any place exists above this point on which tents could be pitched. Perhaps the party will manage without tents, but no great economy of weight will be effected that way; those who sleep out at an elevation of 25,000 or 26,000 feet will have to be bountifully provided with warm things. Probably about fifteen, or at least twelve loads will have to be carried up from Chang La. It is not expected that oxygen will be available for this purpose, and the task, whatever organisation is provided, will be severe, possibly beyond the limits of human strength.

Further, another sort of difficulty will jeopardise the chances of success. It might be possible for two men to struggle somehow to the summit, disregarding every other consideration. It is a different matter to climb the mountain as mountaineers would have it climbed. Principles, time-honoured in the Alpine Club, must of course be respected in the ascent of Mount Everest. The party must keep a margin of safety. It is not to be a mad enterprise rashly pushed on regardless of danger. The ill-considered acceptance of any and every risk has no part in the essence of persevering courage. A mountaineering enterprise may keep sanity and sound judgment and remain an adventure. And of all principles by which we hold the first is that of mutual help. What is to be done for a man who is sick or abnormally exhausted at these high altitudes? His companions must see to it that he is taken down at the first opportunity and with an adequate escort; and the obligation is the same whether he be Sahib or coolie; if we ask a man to carry our loads up the mountain we must care for his welfare at need. It may be taken for granted that such need will arise and will interfere very seriously with any organisation however ingeniously and carefully it may be arranged.

Mount Everest from the 20,000 foot camp—wind blowing snow off the mountain.

In all it may be said that one factor beyond all others is required for success. Too many chances are against the climbers; too many contingencies may turn against them. Anything like a breakdown of the transport will be fatal; soft snow on the mountain will be an impregnable defence; a big wind will send back the strongest; even so small a matter as a boot fitting a shade too tight may endanger one man's foot and involve the whole party in retreat. The climbers must have above all things, if they are to win through, good fortune, and the greatest good fortune of all for mountaineers, some constant spirit of kindness in Mount Everest itself, the forgetfulness for long enough of its more cruel moods; for we must remember that the highest of mountains is capable of severity, a severity so awful and so fatal that the wiser sort of men do well to think and tremble even on the threshold of their high endeavour.

* * *

Published as 'The Reconnaissance of the Mountain'
in *Mount Everest: The Reconnaissance 1921* by C.K. Howard-Bury, 1922, pp 183ff.

7

PURER AIR THAN MORTALS
Mount Everest, 1922

When first the prospect of going to Mount Everest opened for me I used to visualise the expedition in my thoughts as a series of tremendous panting efforts up the final slopes. Later it became a symbol of adventure; I imagined, not so much doing anything of my own will, but rather being led by stupendous circumstances into strange and wonderful situations. Now it has become a problem, with no less interest, and even excitement, the expedition brings to my mind's eye a view of the long mountain slopes set at intervals with groups of little tents, with loads of stores and sleeping sacks, and with men. My object at present is to state this problem—partly because without it the story of our attempts can't well be understood, and partly because the problem is still with us. Everest is not yet climbed. Nor do we know for certain that it can be climbed. But we may see how much nearer we are to a solution as a result of this year's expedition.

The first element in this problem is to supply a camp one stage below the North Col. The reconnaissance of last year had made it plain that this could be done, but it seemed not unlikely with too great a strain; the difficulty is in bringing the porters fresh to this point. General Bruce has proved that this can be done, at all events with his guidance, and we were able to set out this year from our camp at 21,000 feet with full confidence that our porters were in the best of strength and spirits.

The problem of climbing the mountain from that point to the summit, from 21,000 to 29,000 feet, was left after last year's expedition briefly thus: a way to the North Col at 23,000 feet had been found in September, but it was by no means certain that this way would prove convenient, or even serve at all in May and Juno before the monsoon. Upwards from the North Col it was fairly certain that no great obstacle would present itself below the final ridge, and it seemed probable that the true North-eastern ridge to the summit, if it could be reached, would not be insuperable. Our experience in 1921 had also pointed to the period before the monsoon as offering the best chances of favourable weather. In such conditions as prevailed after the monsoon last year it was at all events certain that Mount Everest could not be climbed. Supposing, then, that all the conditions of the mountain should turn out for the best, what were the chances of success? It was known that men could climb to a height of 24,600 feet—the Duke of Abruzzi's record. It was certain, therefore, that they could exist a great deal higher, for the difference between breathing at rest and breathing with the effort of climbing up is immense. My own experience led me to believe that it would be possible to climb at least to 26,000 feet, and probably in one day, from the North Col. But the ultimate limit would be determined, not by a man's capacity when starting fresh on a single day, but when starting on the last of several days after using up his reserves of strength by successive efforts above 21,000 feet; for the reserves are not made good by a night's rest at these great heights. There remained the problem of providing camps to allow the climbers to reach this theoretical limit, or the summit of Mount Everest if the limit were lower than that. It seemed likely that the limit in practice would be determined, not by the endurance of the climbers, but by the capacity of the porters to carry loads above 23,000 feet, and by the organisation of transport within their powers.

Considering this year's expedition with reference to this problem, the climbing party was first concerned with the way up to the North Col. It was obvious to all of us, when we reached the Base Camp and could study the conditions of the mountain, that many of the slopes were icy, even on the North face. Strutt's party returning to the Base Camp on 8 May gave a gloomy account in that respect. The almost level glacier was remarkably icy up to 20,500 feet. Somervell and I, when we went from the Base Camp on 10 May, with orders to act independently and get as high as we could, fully expected prolonged step-cutting up to the North Col. On 13 May we set forth from Camp III with one coolie. Of the slopes which Bullock and I had used in our ascent to the North Col last year, all except the final and steepest one were glittering ice. But we saw that by cutting up a short, steep slope at the bottom we could reach a gently-sloping corridor, and so reach that final slope which was the key to the ascent. Choosing this way we found good snow almost continuously above the first ice. Thus we avoided, not only for that occasion but for the whole of the prolonged assault, a great labour and a great danger. It is essential to have a way up to the North Col where the coolies can very largely look after themselves, and, as it was, the labour of getting up on that first occasion proved quite sufficient.

On the North Col a quite unexpected difficulty arose. The final slope I spoke of gives out on to a wide snow-shelf. Above it is an ice-cliff, broken occasionally by deep fissures. Last year we had easily found a way round this obstacle in the direction of Mount Everest, and so reached the lowest point of the Col. Somervell and I now found this way barred by an impassable crevasse. We stood at the edge of it for a little while, wondering whether it could really be true that we had come so far to be baulked by a crevasse, and debating the use of a ladder. Then we went back and explored in the direction of the North Peak. We found a steep way up at the further end of the ice-cliff, and after leaping two large crevasses proceeded along the hummocky and broken ground beyond; at length we saw a clear way to the level snow from which the North ridge springs. But it does not follow that a party of the future will be so fortunate. One might well be cut off altogether in such a place, which evidently changes a good deal from year to year, and in a country where wood is difficult to obtain another expedition would do well to equip itself against this contingency.

On 13 May, then, we had taken the first step towards establishing Camp IV. The one porter had carried up one tent. Nothing more could be done until more porters were available. Fortunately the transport arrangements below were now working so satisfactorily that on the 15th Strutt, Morshead, and Norton were able to join us at Camp III, and we were able to keep eight coolies from their convoy.

We had now to decide how best under these circumstances to tackle the problem, and principally whether we should attempt to make two camps or only—one above Camp IV at the North Col. The question, when we came to examine it in detail, was practically decided for us; with only nine, or possibly ten, coolies immediately available, the operation of providing a No. VI camp, involving nearly double the labour of providing only Nos IV and V, would take too long, besides in all probability demanding too much of the porters. As it was we had a margin of strength—an invaluable margin. The plan allowed two coolies for each of four loads from Camp IV to Camp V, and it was hoped that by this arrangement they would be able to reach 26,000 feet. The ten more loads were carried to Camp IV, under the North Col, on 17 May.

On the 19th we left camp at 8.45 a.m., carrying up bedding and all warm things available for the porters. The day was fine and sunny. At 1 p.m. Norton and I were putting up tents, while Morshead and Somervell were fixing one more rope between the terrace of our camp and that of the col itself. These domesticities occupied the afternoon, and when sundown came at 4.30 p.m. we turned in for the night, all well and fairly comfortable, proudly possessing six thermos flasks.

Prospects seemed extraordinarily promising. It was our intention to carry on in the morning with only four loads—two of the smallest tents, two double sleeping-sacks, food for one and a half days, cooking pots, and two thermos flasks. Our nine porters, who were housed three apiece in Mummery tents, were perfectly fit, so that we had two porters for each load, even so having a margin of one porter. Everything had been managed so happily and satisfactorily that there was hardly a doubt that the men would be able to establish camp higher up the mountain on the morrow.[18]

Further delays were caused by the cooking operations. It was easy to make tea with the water from our thermos flasks, but we had decided to start the day with a handsome dish of spaghetti. Unfortunately the two tins provided for that purpose, instead of being gently nursed the night long near the warmth of human bodies, had been left out in the cold snow, and edible spaghetti was eventually produced only after prolonged thawing.

We started in the end an hour late, at 7 a.m., quickly making our way to the North Col, whence a broad snow-ridge ascends at a gently increasing angle. It was clear that sooner or later steps would have to be chipped in the hard surface. We were able to avoid this labour at first by following the stone ridge on the West side.

Morshead, if good cheer be a sign of fitness, seemed the strongest and went first; we proceeded at a satisfactory pace in the fine early morning. Perhaps, after all, we should camp at the required height of 26,000 feet.

'Illusory hope of early sun begot!' We presently became aware that it was not a perfect day: the sun had no real warmth, and a cold breeze sprang up from the west. I found myself kicking my toes against the rocks for warmth whenever we paused, and was obliged to put on my spare warm clothes—a Shetland woollie and a silk shirt. The porters were evidently feeling the cold more acutely the higher they went. The ridge of stones ended abruptly, and it became clear that if we were to establish a camp at all, we must race for shelter to the East side of the ridge. Cutting steps at high altitudes is always hard work. The proper way to do it in hard snow is to give one blow with the ice-axe and then stamp the foot into the hole just made; but such a blow requires a man's full strength, and he must kick hard into the hole. On the higher Himalayas the amateur will probably prefer to make two or three chips of a feebler sort in cutting his steps. In any case, 300 feet of such work, particularly if hurried, is extremely exhausting, and we were glad to rest at length about noon, sheltered under rocks at about 25,000 feet.

There was no question now of getting our loads much higher before camping. The porters would have to return to camp; it would have been an unwarrantable risk to expose them further in such conditions; they must be sent down before they were frost-bitten and before the weather could change for the worse. Under other conditions it might have been necessary for some of us to accompany them on their way down; now they could safely be sent alone. No camping-place could be seen where we were, so we crossed round to the sheltered side, vaguely hoping that one might present itself. Eventually the porters with Somervell professed to have found the right place, and on the steep mountain side they proceeded to build a wall of stones so as to construct a comparatively flat place for one of the Mummery tents.

Norton and I, feebly imitating their efforts, proceeded to erect another, but somehow in our case the walls did not serve. One site after another proved a failure, until at last we found a steep slab of rock, which was at all events in itself secure, and so placed that it was possible to make up the ground at its lower end. Here we ultimately pitched our tent in such a way that the slab took up half the floor-space. A more uncomfortable arrangement could not have been devised, as the inevitable result was that one man slid down on to the other as they lay, squeezing them tightly together, and so increasing almost to the pitch of agony the pain caused by the sharp rocks forming the other part of the floor.

There, however, were the two little tents, perched fifty yards apart, in some sort of fashion for security under the lee of rocks, containing each a double sleeping-bag for warmth in the night. Somervell melted snow with much labour for a perfunctory meal, and soon each bag harboured a pair of men, tightly packed, warming each other, and warmed by the prospect full of hope of a day's mountaineering unlike all others, because we were to start from a point on the earth's surface higher than any before reached.

Perhaps none of us yet realised how much we had already suffered from the cold. Norton's ear was thrice its normal size, and proved a considerable inconvenience by limiting the number of admissible dispositions for his limbs and mine in those close quarters. Three of my fingers were frost-touched; but luckily the effects of frostbite are not very serious in the early stages. Far more serious was Morshead's condition. Too late in the day he had put on his sledging suit for protection against the wind; on arriving in camp he was chilled and evidently unwell. We had also to regret the loss of Norton's rucksack; it slipped from his knees during a halt, and must now lie somewhere at the head of the Rongbuk Glacier with its provision of warm things for the night; however, we still had enough among us.

Our chief anxiety was the weather; the west wind dropped in the evening, and the signs pointed to a change. At intervals during the night we noticed that stars were visible; nearer dawn we were disgusted to observe that the ground outside was snow-white. A little later, listening, we heard fine hail falling on the tents, and peering out of the tent door it was possible to make out that the cloud and mist were coming up from the East on a monsoon current.

At 6.30 a.m., with somewhat better signs, we extricated ourselves from our sleeping-bags and set about preparing a meal. Only one thermos flask had turned up overnight, so that our task was cold and long. Another ill-fated rucksack containing provisions slipped from our perch, but miraculously, after bounding a hundred feet or more, stopped on a small ledge. Morshead, heroically exerting himself, recovered it.

At about 8 o'clock we were ready to start. We did not discuss whether under these conditions we ought to proceed. The snow which had fallen was obviously an impediment, and more was to be expected. But weather of this sort, with all its disadvantages to the mountaineer, may not mean mischief. In high altitudes the snow falls fine, and is not hard driven by the wind. So far as getting up was concerned, there was therefore little fear on this count. None of us, after a long, headachy night, felt at our best. For my part, I hoped that the mere effort at deep breathing in the first few steps of the ascent would string me up to the required efforts, and that we all should be better once we had started.

Disappointment followed at the moment of setting out in hearing bad news from Morshead: 'I think I won't come with you,' he said; 'I am quite sure I should only keep you back.'

On such a question only the man concerned is able to judge. We three [Mallory, Somervell, and Norton] went on regretfully without him.

Details of the climbing of the next few hours do not merit exact description. The conditions were naturally unfavourable: fresh snow covered the ledges and concealed loose stones, everywhere obstructive; but the general nature of the ground was not difficult. Despite the geological conjectures of last year, we did not find ourselves climbing chimneys and flakes. There was no sign of granite as we stepped up from ledge to ledge; and these ledges were uniformly tilted disadvantageously.

Plainly the rock is of a stratified sedimentary form, and as far as can be shown it must have the same general nature up to the summit, varied only by recognisable bands of lighter-coloured quartzite. It was a disappointment that the angle of the ledge was not sufficiently steep to require a more strenuous use of the arms, for the arms help one up, seeming to relieve the monotony of balanced footwork.

It was a matter of slowly pushing up, first regaining the ridge by striking westwards, then following the ridge itself directly towards the great tower capping the North-east shoulder of the mountain. Ultimately, the power of pushing up depended upon lung capacity. Lungs governed our speed, making the pace a miserable crawl. From the Alpine point of view our lungs made us pause to admire the view oftener than is correct in the best circles. But our lungs were remarkably alike and went well together. Personally I contrived a looseness of the muscles by making an easy, deep-drawn breath, and by exercising deep breathing I found myself able to proceed. For a long time we had good hope of reaching the North-east shoulder, but, remembering the long descent to be made and the retarding circumstances of fresh snow, we agreed to turn back not much later than 2 p.m.

We had to consider Morshead left behind at Camp V. On his account it was desirable to get back to camp with time in hand to reach the North Col on the same day; and in any case it would be an insane risk to climb to the utmost limit of one's strength on Mount Everest and trust to inspiration or brandy to get one down in safety; for the body does not recover strength in the descent as it does in the Alps.

At 2.15, some time after crossing the head of a conspicuous couloir on the North-east face, we reached, as it were, the head of the rocks, still perhaps 500 feet below the North-east shoulder of the mountain, and commanding a clear view to the summit. The pace of the party was extremely slow, and there was obvious risk in spending much more time in going up. Greatly as we desired to gain the shoulder—and we were not yet at the end of our powers—the only wisdom was in retreat. The aneroid registered 26,800 feet. We turned to descend with sufficient strength, we believed, for the long task before us.

Away to the westward the ground appeared to be less rocky, and to have more snow. Our obvious plan was to make use of any snow-slope in that direction for our descent. We were, however, very quickly disillusioned, as the 'snow-slopes' turned out to be a series of slabs of rock lying treacherously under a fresh white mask of snow. We were obliged to get back to our ridge and follow down along our upward tracks. At 4 o'clock Morshead welcomed us back to our camp of the previous night at 25,000 feet. After gathering what we wanted and leaving our tents, sleeping-sacks, and other items, we proceeded back along the ledge which our track of yesterday had followed. It was difficult to realise immediately how the freshly-fallen snow had made of this easy ground a dangerous passage. A nasty slip occurred, and three men were held only by the rope secured round the leader's single ice-axe. The party proceeded very cautiously after this incident, and it soon became evident that it would be a race with the on-coming darkness.

When we regained the great snow-ridge, no traces of the steps we had cut on the upward journey could be found; we had to repeat the step-cutting. That grim and slow process was observed at about 6 o'clock by Strutt from below in Camp III. Nor were our difficulties at an end after the passage of this slope. One of the disagreeable facts which differentiates Himalayan expeditions from those in lower mountains is that an exhausted man does not recover his strength quickly as he goes down. Morshead, although climbing very pluckily and making the most tremendous efforts to get his breath, had now arrived at the end of his tether. At best he could only proceed a few steps at a time. Fortunately, it was easy going on the way down to the North Col as we watched the diminishing light.

Norton supported Morshead with his shoulder while I was finding the easiest way down, and Somervell acted as rear-guard. Lightning from blue-grey sinister clouds to the west began to flicker after sunset over one of the most amazing mountain views and one which seemed to be full of malice. What sort of wind were we going to find on the Col after dark when our difficulties were due to begin once more?

Our luck was good, or Providence was kind, for, as soon as we had arrived at the starlit crevasses now dimly confronting us and Somervell had produced the lantern from his rucksack, so calm was the air that even with a Japanese match, after a dozen trials or so, we lit our candle. By its light we groped hither and thither to find our way; there were crevasses concealed beneath the trackless surfaces; happily no one fell through before we reached the edge of a little cliff. Here it was necessary to jump down about 15 feet into snow, a sufficiently alarming prospect with so dim a light to guide one; but the leap was safely accomplished. One of the fixed ropes, if only we could find it, would now take us down to the terrace where the five tents could just be seen still neatly pitched in a row awaiting our arrival. The rope had become buried by snow and our last candle burnt out. We groped for some time along the edge of the precipice and then began to go down at a steep angle, doubting whether this were the way. Suddenly someone hooked up the rope from under the snow. We knew then that we could reach the tents.

A little later, at 11.30, we were searching our camp for fuel and cooking-pots. None were found. A meal without liquid food was not to be contemplated; but the North Col, unless snow could be melted, was 'dry'. The best 'ersatz', invented by Norton, was a mixture of jam and snow with frozen condensed milk. The sickly stuff was most unlike a drink, and I ascribe to its influence the uncontrollable shudderings, spasms of muscular contraction in belly and back which I suffered in my sleeping-bag, and which caused me to sit up and inhale again great whiffs from the night air, as though that habit of deep breathing had settled upon me indispensably.

On the following morning, urged still by our unrelieved cravings, we set off at 6 a.m. I suppose a fresh man with tracks to help him might comfortably reach Camp III in an hour from the North Col. It took us six hours, and we worked hard; we had to make a staircase beneath the new snow good enough for porters' use, for we did not intend to sleep at 21,000 feet without our sleeping-bags. And it is worth remarking that the circumstance of new snow and covered tracks must always be a serious consideration to a tired party on Chang La.

In the light of these experiences we may review afresh the problem of climbing Mount Everest. By far the most important modification of our previous view is in respect of the porters. Their power was far greater than was to be expected. None before had ever carried a camp above 23,500 feet; these men carried our loads to 25,000; Finch's even higher to 25,500 feet, and some of them even repeated this amazing feat on three successive days. Nor is there the smallest reason to suppose that after sleeping a night above 25,000 feet they would be incapable of going on next day. They showed astonishingly little signs of fatigue. The mountain-sickness to which some of them succumbed on the North Col was easily accounted for by the fact that they closed their tent doors and slept with too little air; nothing of the kind occurred again. The fact that the porters were capable of so much and endured so well has profoundly altered the aspect of our problem. It seems that almost certainly a sixth camp, at about 27,000 feet, might be carried up; and the limit of climbing, instead of being determined by the difficulty of fixing camps, will be determined simply by the factor of endurance among the trained climbers.

And what, after this year's performances, may be expected of them? It will have been observed that the three of us who reached 26,800 feet[19] climbed only 1,800 feet in a day from our camp; but the maximum time was not available; bad weather delayed our start, and the descent was to a camp below our starting-point. So far as time is concerned we should have had five hours more, and judging by the party's performance up to their highest point, I haven't the smallest doubt that with five hours more 700 feet might have been added to the record, and the day's performance brought to 2,500 feet. The question, then, which I should put is this: Is it conceivable, in the first place, that in two days above the North Col a camp could be fixed at 27,000 feet? And, in the second, supposing a party to start from 27,000 feet, could they conceivably climb in a day the remaining 2,000 feet to the summit? We cannot, of course, give a certain answer; but at all events the question does not appear fantastic. The effort of climbing the last 2,000 feet to the summit should not in itself be considerably greater than that of climbing the 2,000 feet from 25,000 to 27,000; for the difference in atmospheric pressure is very small, only .8 of an inch between 27,000 feet to the summit, compared with a difference of 19½ inches between sea-level and 27,000 feet. The factors which will tell against the climber on this last section are his efforts on the previous days, from which it may be supposed he will not have recovered completely, and, possibly, ill-effects from sleeping at these very high camps. But if any gambler has been laying odds on the mountain, he should very considerably reduce his ratio as a result of this year's expedition.

I imagine that a number of physiologists, especially, would be inclined to reduce these odds on the mountain. I was told at Oxford last year, by Sir Walter Raleigh, that the physiologists said it was physiologically impossible to climb to the top of Mount Everest without oxygen—the matter had been proved by experiments in a pressure-reducing chamber. I told Sir Walter that the physiologists might explode themselves in their diabolical chamber, but we would do what we could to explode their damnable heresy—or words to that effect. I always, as a matter of course, take off my hat to scientists, as latter-day Olympians breathing a different if not purer air than common mortals. But the air of Mount Olympus (a base little lump after all) is not that of Mount Everest, and experiments made there with a pumped-out tank, interesting as they may be, are of no value in determining where precisely on that other hill of unrivalled altitude persevering man will be brought to a standstill; for it must be supposed of the persevering man that he has been acclimatised to rarefied air, while the Olympian and other victims of those experiments are only acclimatised to the atmosphere of Mount Olympus, which, I am given to understand, is particularly dense. Acclimatisation—this is the factor at the root of the matter. The best experiment in this respect is to go to Mount Everest, or some other high mountain, and see how you feel; the scientists may explain your feelings, but when it comes to prophecy they have less right to be heard than a high-climbing mountaineer; the idea of the man who has tried as to how much higher he might go should be of incomparably more value than any conclusion proceeding mere- ly from a laboratory. The best opinion on this question must surely be that of Somervell (may he forgive me for bringing his name into this controversial matter), who, besides climbing to 26,985 feet (accepting the theodolite figure as against the aneroid) without the aid of oxygen, has a trained knowledge of physiology. I think he will not disagree with any remarks of mine on this subject.

We have considered so far only the problem of climbing Mount Everest without oxygen. To climb the mountain with oxygen is a separate problem; here Finch is the authority, and it is not my province to discuss the details. It will be remembered that Somervell and I when we went up for the third attempt this year intended to use oxygen; judging from what had been said by Finch, Bruce, and others too who had used oxygen up to the North Col, we imagined we should go further with than without it. It was this possibility that decided us during that long day of 4 June while we lay in the sangar at Camp I, watching the clouds and the snow, to push up again—to be repelled finally by some danger that we ought not to face or to be conquered by the difficulties. The problem of climbing Mount Everest with the aid of oxygen seemed not so very far beyond our powers, provided the fair opportunity, when we thought of what had been done already. Perhaps the most significant fact was this—that three of us, after climbing to a height only about 2000 feet below the summit, had felt no special distress.

Two other considerations must engage our attention, because they affect the problem of climbing Mount Everest, the dangers involved, and the weather. This year's expedition has emphasised the dangers. It has tragically pointed to the danger of an avalanche on the way up to the North Col—how grievous an accident it was can only be known to those who had tested those seven brave men, had contact with their gay indomitable spirits, seen their unflagging good humour, received tokens of their constant will to help, of their unfailing, faithful hearts. An impartial judge may say that in the last analysis the accident was due to imperfect knowledge of snow in this part of the Himalayas; and, with the comment that one never can know enough about snow, I should bow to that judgment. The lesson at all events will not be forgotten, and one may suppose that another party will not be caught in the same way.

About the other dangers it is necessary to say more because they must vitally affect the organisation of any attempt to climb the mountain. Everyone will remember how Morshead's collapse compromised our plan of descent. There is, of course, no question of his determination; his companions have nothing but sympathy for him and praise for his splendid pluck. The causes of this collapse are obscure; his heart was not affected; possibly it was due to want of liquid food. At starting from the North Col Morshead seemed fitter than anyone; his failure was a complete surprise to all of us; and in view of it I think a party of the future should reckon that some such experience may happen to any one of them. At a high altitude even the strongest might suffer this loss of muscular power; and *he will not recover up there*. The danger in such a case can hardly be over-estimated; all calculations of time will be upset, and the awful fate of a night out, perhaps above 27,000 feet, will be hanging over the party. The only valid precaution against such an event is to have another party in reserve at the camp from which the first climbers have started.

Another danger, to which I referred last year, concerns the porters. It must be remembered that, though active men, they are not trained mountaineers. In favourable conditions they would probably climb down, say, from 26,000 feet without disaster. Even so, this practice is not to be commended; they are apt to straggle, and have no idea of looking after one another. And they are averse to using a rope. But on the crevassed North Col the rope must be used for safety; and conditions are not always favourable. As a general rule provision should be made to escort the porters, even when tracks are available. And this, again, points to a much larger personnel, capable of effective action at least up to 25,000 feet.

It may further be said, though it must be obvious to any mountaineer, that at high altitudes one climbs much nearer the margin of strength. There is singularly little reserve for an emergency, though I'm glad to say there was enough for emergencies in the case of the climb I have described. It is not too much to assert that all dangers through faults in climbing are immensely greater on Mount Everest than, for instance, on Mount Blanc or the Matterhorn.

Again, the sum of all these dangers is increased to an extent that cannot be over-emphasised by unfavourable weather. A party with one man *hors de combat,* a party who have passed that indefinite line beyond which more weakness becomes a danger, a party of porters with no tracks to guide them and no compass lore, or finding fresh snow on the steep slope below the North Col: men in such circumstances are in gravest peril when the wind blows on Mount Everest. It is when we view our problem as a whole, in the light of the weather experienced this year, that we should be least inclined to optimism. Apart from any consideration of the monsoon's date, and that of 1922 was admittedly early, the conditions before it came were not encouraging. The weather had a bad habit; it presented us with a dilemma; either we might have a taste of the monsoon and the threat of snow in the air—it will be remembered that snow fell while we were encamped at 25,000 feet—or we should have that bitter enemy, the North-west wind, the wind that drove us to camp a thousand feet lower than we intended, the wind that Finch and Bruce will not forget for its howling during the first night at their high camp.

Perhaps it is not impossible for men to reach the summit of Mount Everest, in spite of wind and weather; but unless the weather can mend the habit we observed this year, or grant a long respite, their chances of reaching it and getting down in safety are all too small. Man may calculate how to solve his problem, and... you may finish the sentence.

* * *

Read before the Joint Meeting of the Alpine Club and the Royal Geographical Society, 16 October, 1922, published as 'The Second Mount Everest Expedition' *Alpine Journal*, Vol 34, 1922, pp 425ff.

8

EVEREST UNVANQUISHED
Mount Everest, 1922

The sensation of coming up to Tibet from the Chumbi Valley, from the country of flowers and butterflies, of streams and meadows, of rich greens on the hillsides and of deep blue atmospheres, the regret of leaving all that has delighted the senses and exchanging it in one short march for everything that is dreary is one of the most poignant experiences that I remember. The mere absence of wood is from the most practical point of view a great loss; the alternative fuel is yak-dung, which makes a hotter fire but requires constant blowing and is less convenient for cooking. The regrets of one who looks out over the treeless plains and knows what is in store for him will probably be concerned with less practical issues: when the pungent smoke of a yak-dung fire first meets his nostrils, or the actual taste of it, which permeates all food, is bitter on his palate, he will remember the sweet flavour of blue wood-smoke; when his cracked skin meets the cold, dry wind blowing mercilessly day after day for ten or twelve hours, he will have a thought for the soft airs of Sikkim where he perspired so pleasantly; and when the dust blows up, and his ears and hair are full of it, and his neck gritty to touch, and everything he possesses mixed with dust, oh, then he will long for one of those warm streams in some forest gorge where he washed and washed his sticky body.

As a man comes up this way, his first midday view of the Tibetan plains must chill the most passionate ardour for travel, even travel to the top of Mount Everest—these grim plains undulating interminably to bare hills and forbidding snow mountains. And yet, standing on a mound rising out of the plain near Phari Dzong, before sunset, when shadows fill the folds on the sunlit hillsides, or after sunset, when the wind has dropped and the vast expanse is gathered and waits for the common fate of darkness, then he may learn that even Tibet has a heart and a moving spirit. And if next morning he is on the calm plain early, he may see the glory of Chomolhari rising 10,000 feet above him, fresh-clothed in sunlight, and he may expect each morning of the journey to see some new wonder.

The object of climbing Mount Everest is sufficient for a mountaineer. He cannot make an image in his mind of the world's highest mountain, the 'Goddess Mother of the Country,' as the natives call it, raised in splendour on that remote frontier between Nepal and Tibet, without being moved to the desire of reaching the summit; in the very fact that it remains unconquered he sees a challenge. To accept this challenge was the first and moving thought in the Alpine Club and the Royal Geographical Society when the Everest Committee was appointed by these two bodies to organise an expedition. At the same time the climbing-parties did not forget scientific interests, and they wished to give for the purposes of science an accurate account of their experiences.

A reconnaissance of the mountain was the special task of the Alpine Club contingent in the First Expedition, May to October, 1921, under the leadership of Colonel C.K. Howard-Bury. Unfortunately two of our party were already out of action before Colonel Howard-Bury had brought us to the mountain and it was left to two others of us to do what we could. Guy Bullock, my companion, was an old school friend and our climbing together had begun on the ancient walls and roofs of Winchester College. He and I moved our little tent about the valleys of Everest for many weeks between June and September. We decided that the four main ridges and the four main faces that lie between them were all, singly considered, impossible to climb at these altitudes. But the upper part of the Northeast Ridge looked hopeful above the point called the North-east Shoulder, at 27,400 feet, that is, 1,600 feet below the summit. At this point the North-east Ridge is joined by a subsidiary arm, the North Ridge, which we decided could be climbed. The only access to it is by way of a snow-saddle called the North Col, which joins the North Ridge with the North Peak. It was finally proved by the practical experiment of getting there that we could reach the North Col. This point was the limit of our endeavour in 1921.

The Second Expedition, March to July, 1922, made three attempts to reach the summit of the mountain. Twelve Europeans under the leadership of General C.G. Bruce set out from Darjeeling on 26 March. The route of 1921 was followed as far as Shekar Dzong, where we turned south to reach the Rongbuk Valley, the northern approach to Mount Everest. Here at a height of 16,300 feet, a little below the foot of the glacier, the base camp was established. The animals could go no higher and the stores collected there had to be taken thenceforward on men's backs. Not all thirteen of our party expected to reach great heights—not General Bruce, nor Colonel Strutt, second in command, and a well-known and active alpinist, nor Dr. Longstaff, our medical officer and the one among us who had most experience of the Himalaya; younger men are required. Captain Noel, our photographer, had other work to do; Captain Morris and Mr Crawford were primarily transport officers, destined to be vitally important links between the base camp and the higher camps on the mountain. Seven only might be expected to be high climbers.

The journey from Darjeeling was in itself a large part of what had to be accomplished. To enter Tibet it is necessary first to pass through the small protected state of Sikkim, which may roughly be described as a jumble of gigantic foot-hills for the most part covered by subtropical vegetation. The British authorities had the greatest difficulty in finding animals which could endure both the warm, moist heat in the valleys of Sikkim and the dry cold of Tibet at elevations above 14,000 feet. Buffaloes and camels from India and Tibetan yaks were alike unable to support the violent changes of climate; disease broke out among them and thousands died of anthrax or rinderpest. Only one animal was suitable for our task, the mule. It was with a hundred government mules from India that the First Expedition started from Darjeeling in 1921. But even mules will not stand the strain of marching up and down the steep ridges of Sikkim unless they have been previously trained. The government mules which looked so sleek and well at the start broke down after a few marches. Fortunately we were able to hire Tibetan mules in their place. These animals are constantly engaged on the wool trade, carrying Tibetan wool down to India and usually going back unladen. Accustomed as they are to the steep, slippery paths, they will go on for many hours faster than a man can walk and make nothing of ascending 5,000 feet and coming down another 5,000 feet on the same day with loads of 120 or even 150 pounds on their backs. Up to Phari, the Tibetan mules also solved the problem of transport for General Bruce in 1922.

Beyond Phari, where we left the trade route, we found it a formidable matter to keep ourselves and our baggage moving. The magic touch was provided by a pass from the Dalai Lama at Lhasa, which the Government of India had procured for us and which we showed to the local governors, or dzongpens, wherever we went. There was much ceremony about these meetings with dzongpens, visits on both sides and presents and palaver. Eventually the dzongpen would summon the head-men of neighbouring villages and requisition from them the animals we wanted. With them we should be able to continue our journey so far as the domain of the next dzongpen. The price, too, was fixed in consultation with him. It was all very complicated and difficult to arrange; for some of the animals would come on only one day's march to the next village, while others would continue for several stages. Colonel Howard-Bury found out very well how to travel in Tibet. Perhaps in 1921 the Tibetans were more afraid of us and helped us for that reason, while in 1922 they had learned that we were there to pay good money and helped us more because it was profitable.

It was certainly very important that they should be disposed to help us in 1922, for we required 360 animals to carry our loads each day, and had General Bruce been willing to go on at any stage with less than all our loads, we should have been involved in endless delays. When I think of those barren plains in April of last year before the summer sun had thawed the grazing-camps and caused the grass to spring, it is almost inconceivable that we could have travelled across them with so many loads. I see the animals, now, scattering over the plains in a broken line; groups of little donkeys carrying burdens as large as themselves, and—one or another of them—occasionally sinking to the ground for a short stop by way of protest; persistent, shaggy, imperturbable yaks, moving faster than appears and always first in camp, and a heterogeneous collection of bullocks having more or less of the yak or cow nature, heavy, slow-moving beasts. And what in the wide world are these animals going to eat this night? It turns out, when we reach the grazing-camp, that they actually feed on nothing at all but the brown stubble of coarse grass or the roots thereof.

My admiration is forever divided between the yak and the donkey, but I have no doubt as to which is more interesting. Docile and amiable at most times, the yak is a temperamental creature. He is subject to moments of exuberance. For no discernible cause he will suddenly go wild and rush madly about, kicking out his heels and trying to get rid of his load. And not quite in earnest, like a child half angry and ready to laugh, the yak seems to know that this is a comic turn. There is a strange contrast between his normal, steady gait and his agility at need. His usual pace over moderately rough ground is 24 miles per hour; he will go at this rate all day even without a midday feed if properly driven—that is, if he has stones thrown at him, not maliciously but dexterously, for his guidance. If anyone tries to press him to a faster pace, he will invariably shoot off at right angles to the line of march. Pressing, in fact, is punished as in golf and nothing is easier than to slice a yak. His agility is even more amazing in difficult country. I have known loaded yaks to climb rocks where a man could not get up without using his arms, and I shall never forget the ludicrous figures they cut, these cumbrous, shaggy beasts with mild, liquid eyes protesting as they proceeded in rushes from ledge to ledge as though imitating the slim chamois.

The yak-drivers are the finest men in Tibet, competent, faithful, enduring. I confess that I made few friends in this country. I do not know that it was because they were unwashed that I usually found the Tibetans unattractive. After all there is little incentive to wash in that dry, cold climate; I can well imagine that instead of washing my body once in three or four weeks I might come with a longer stay to making a bath only an annual midsummer event. The peasants I thought would have pleased me better if they had shown us less of their silly gaping air as they stood about our tents agog with curiosity, and I judged them to lack virility. The men of substance, who owned beasts and with whom the price of transport was commonly the question of moment, seemed very hard and avaricious and unhelpful unless immediately under the eye of a dzongpen; but they were honest in that they kept the letter of their bond though willing to practise all sorts of deception about the way and the distance of some stage of our journey. The lamas in the monasteries contained among them an occasional man of real force and ability, and even, I imagine, of rich spiritual experience, but the great majority seemed even more silly than the peasants and disgusted one's nostrils with their smell of rancid butter.

The journey to Mount Everest took between four and five weeks from Darjeeling. Of course the pilgrims passed their time more in talking than anything else. This was particularly true of the Second Expedition. When the experiences of thirteen men most of whom have travelled not a little, are pooled, they multiply indefinitely. But not all of every day was occupied in travelling and talking. According to our various interests we were fairly busy in camp after the tents had been pitched. Most of us took up a preposterous amount of time merely in finding what we wanted even from our own kits. The days of rest which we were obliged to take while fresh transport was collected, were easily spent. The country near the camp must be explored for birds and beasts and plants and for the mere interest of the views from available hilltops. The principal activity, however, in such a camp was photography. One or two of us found time to write letters home, but correspondence was usually postponed until the General announced that runners would be sent back with mail on the following day. Then the idle murmur about our tents was hushed while everyone feverishly scribbled.

In 1921 when the units of the expedition separated for their different purposes, there was little common life in the mess. But in 1922 we were all engaged on one task and though of course split up into parties for transport and climbing, we had a good deal of time to spend at the base camp and our mess there was as gay and pleasant as can well be imagined. The food supplies had been provided by the Everest Committee on the assumption that the chosen stalwarts who were to assault Mount Everest would have appetites becoming the heroes of old. It was desirable that we should be generously fed like anyone else who is training his body to be fit for a supreme physical effort. It may be agreed that when a climber arrives at the base camp, he should be well-covered rather than lean—not finely trained, since he will have to draw so much on his reserves later on. Perhaps the most valuable of our supplies were hams, cheeses and canned milk. There was much besides: soups, vegetables, fish and meat in innumerable tins and, especially for high altitudes, spaghetti and a variety of sweetmeats, chocolate, mint-cake (pure sugar flavoured with mint), acid drops, ginger, raisins and prunes. The duty of dealing with mess-stores was finally taken over by Major Norton as mess-president with two assistants, Somervell and Crawford. After a few days they became extraordinarily quick at recognising our countless pieces of baggage, and the apparently hopeless task of finding any particular box in the heap was brought within practicable limits.

Many hours of this Second Expedition must have been spent by all of us simply in checking our stores, taking stock of the amazing bales and boxes carried each day on the backs of so many beasts. But we were not all concerned with all the boxes. Noel, for instance, had his own contingent carrying photographic material, about 40 animal-loads. Finch had special charge of the oxygen equipment; 120 steel cylinders weighing each six pounds, pumped up to a pressure of 120 atmospheres and containing 120 litres of oxygen; and besides the cylinders twelve sets of apparatus for using the gas. The oxygen apparatus consisted of a steel frame to carry four cylinders on the back, a copper tube conveying the gas over the shoulder to the reducing valve and various taps which were to regulate the supply of rubber tubing to a mask fitted on the climber's face. Since these were delicate instruments, they were packed in wooden cases and twelve Tibetan coolies were always secured to carry them.

My own concern was more particularly with alpine stores. We had two sorts of light tent for the high camps. Each kind had a ground-sheet sewn into the sides, the most wind-proof arrangement, and was made of specially treated 'wing-fabric', which is very strong but not very light. Including the poles but leaving out of account the flies, which we did not intend to take very high, the smaller tent weighed about eleven pounds and the larger fifteen pounds for a floor seven feet square. Our sleeping-bags were lined with flannel, stuffed with eiderdown and covered with a water-proofed material and were made up some to take two and others three men. There were 2,000 feet of climbing-rope. Not the least important items in our climbing-equipment were the different fuels, stoves and pots for high altitudes. For the Primus stoves, to be used chiefly between 18,000 and 22,000 feet, we took along a mixture of paraffin and petrol. We had also two precious gallons of alcohol to serve both for lighting the Primus stoves and for burning at the highest altitudes in a spirit-burner; and, as a final reserve, a solidi-fied spirit of exceptional purity called Meta, the white cylinders of which can be lighted and will burn without smoke at least as high as 25,000 feet.

Apart from each man's personal supply of clothing there were large reserves of specially warm articles such as gloves, socks and helmets, and two big boxes of experimental foot-gear. Nothing is more difficult than to provide boots suitable at the same time to keep the feet warm in snow at exceedingly low temperatures and to climb on both snow and rocks. The nails ordinarily used by alpine climbers conduct heat away from the feet, and anything in the nature of crampons (steel frames with spikes) would be still more dangerous because the straps binding them on the foot tend to stop circulation. The various moccasins, felt boots spiked sandals, etc., though of admirable service for keeping our feet warm in camp, were all rejected in favour of ordinary alpine boots with special nails.

Important as equipment is, no other single factor in the ultimate success of any plan to climb the highest mountain in the Himalaya counts for so much as the fashion in which porters are used to establish high camps. It would be possible of course, though very expensive, to take out from the alpine valleys of Switzerland or Italy or France porters accustomed to mountaineering. But one finds it simpler, particularly when arranging for food supplies, to employ natives. The best, and probably no sturdier men could be found, are the Sherpa Bhutias, a tribe living in Nepal at no great distance from Mount Everest. Both expeditions took a number of these men. The one difficulty about them is that they are not trained mountaineers. In 1921 Bullock and I tried to get over this difficulty by systematic training of them. A number of them learnt something about the game and could be relied upon to step firmly and upright in snow or ice-steps and even to help each other at times with the rope, though they were much slower in picking up this end of the business.

The work done by our porters in 1921 was prodigious. After carrying loads through Tibet, they had three months, off and on, of living in high camps and reaching altitudes above 20,000 feet, though not able to get just the food they wanted when we were away from the main body. Their final achievement was to come up with Bullock, Wheeler and me one day late in September to the North Col (23,000 feet). But only three of them came with us and they carried no loads. To establish a camp on the North Col then was almost certainly beyond our strength; it was as much as most of the porters could do to crawl back over the pass we had crossed. The question therefore for 1922 was, so to manage the porters that they could carry up our camp not only to the North Col, but one or two stages higher.

The season chosen for the enterprise was the month of May. It must be borne in mind that all this region of the Himalaya is subject to the influence of the monsoon which blows up from the south-east, bringing rain to north-eastern India and snow to the mountains throughout the summer. We intended to climb before the monsoon. We chose the early season rather than the late, chiefly as a result of our experience after the monsoon in 1921. Then, so soon as the weather had cleared on Mount Everest, the prevailing northwest wind of Tibet had come up and the fresh, powdery snow was blown in unbroken spindrift across the face of the mountain. If we must encounter this bitter wind, we would rather have it without the blown snow.

General Bruce's plan with regard to the porters was to save them for the climax. From the start in Darjeeling they carried no loads up to the base camp; they were almost extravagantly fed and splendidly equipped with boots and clothes. They were childishly delighted with these new vanities; they felt that everything was being done for them and, when the time came to call upon them for supreme efforts, they were ready and eager to respond. But only forty were available for carrying on our loads up the glacier when we had sent down the animals from the base camp.

Our procedure after we established this camp at 16,300 feet, on 1 May, may be understood to have had three phases: first, the supplying of Camp III, an advanced base at 21,000 feet, which would serve as a jumping-off place for any party attempting to reach the summit (this was known as Camp III because two staging camps, I and II, were required below it, and the work of moving up stores along this chain continued simultaneously with activities higher up); secondly, the carrying of a comparatively small quantity of stores, but still a larger quantity than we should immediately use, up to Camp IV, situated on a protected shelf not far from the foot of the North Ridge and only just below the edge of that snowy saddle known in Tibetan as the Chang La, in English as the North Col (this work could begin as soon as Camp III was sufficiently supplied and porters, released from their labours below this camp, were available for going higher); thirdly, the attempts to reach the summit, after a start from Camp IV with just what was required but no more. All these camps were permanent in the sense that the tents, once pitched, remained *in situ*; but since we had not a complete double set of sleeping-bags, some of these had to be moved up and down.

It will be seen that much moving of stores was necessary before we could start for the summit. And only a limited time was available.

We learned from the lamas at the Rongbuk Monastery that the monsoon should be expected about 10 June. In order to hurry up the second phase, to free some of our Nepalese porters as soon as possible for work above Camp III, General Bruce demanded the cooperation of Tibetans. But Tibetans have no love for this sort of work. Ninety were requisitioned; forty-five turned up. These worked for two days. On the third morning none appeared. We learned that they had returned to their own villages four or five marches away. With the weather-signs pointing to an early, rather than a late, monsoon our chief was determined to have something done quickly, and with that object sent up only two of us, Somervell and me, on 10 May. On 12 May we reached Camp III.

At the base camp, meanwhile, other Tibetans were coming in, willing to work for the high wages, and on 15 May a convoy reached Camp III with Colonel Strutt, Norton and Morshead. It was time to be making a definite plan of attack. The initial attempt was to be made without the help of oxygen. We wanted to try only ordinary means first, and besides we did not intend to waste several days of fine weather in waiting till the cylinders could be brought up. Probably the best chance of attaining the summit of Mount Everest is to make three stages of the 6,000 feet above the North Col, from 23,000 to 29,000 feet, and to launch the final assault with a party of four climbers from a camp at about 27,000 feet. We soon decided now that four of us should go on, Morshead, Norton, Somervell and I. But at present only ten porters could be spared from work at lower stages, and it would be as much as they could do without too long delay to establish Camp IV on the North Col and one more above it. The best we could hope for our final camp would be a height of 26,000 feet.

On 19 May we slept at Camp IV with nine porters. We intended to carry on in the morning only four loads—two light tents, two double sleeping-sacks, provisions for a day and a half and some thermos flasks—so that we should have two porters to each load and even so one to spare. Early next morning, when I attempted to rouse the porters, I found them not all well, probably because they had tightly closed their tents during the night. Five were suffering from mountain-sickness.

The four remaining porters sufficed to establish Camp V. But the bitter northwest gale had driven us over on the lee side of the mountain. Norton had an ear frost-bitten, and I myself three fingertips, while Morshead had suffered beyond calculation from a severe chill; and our camp after all was a thousand feet lower than we had hoped. It was a miserable place, too, in which to spend the night; for there was no sufficient flat space for a tent. We had the one consolation that at 25,000 feet we were higher than any climbing-party had been before.

During the night the wind dropped and snow began to fall. The early morning seemed hopeless. But by eight o'clock we had had breakfast and the weather was clear enough. But when we had gone only a few paces, Morshead stopped and told us he would not come on. He felt certain he could not go far and he was only anxious not to keep us back. We left him in camp and plodded wearily on, each man starting, after the cramped and aching night, more tired than he had been the night before. It was not a matter of very difficult climbing, of hanging on by finger-tips and toes. The problem was rather to keep up just the mean pace that would not too rapidly exhaust us; we must breathe in the first instance with the full power of our lungs so that our limbs might be induced to put themselves in motion; we must 'keep our form' as oarsmen say, 'at the end of the race', proceeding not with violent rushes but with even, balanced movements, stepping neatly and helping ourselves with our arms. In this way we were able to push on, though slowly. The question as to whether we should reach the top this day would be decided by the two factors, *pace* and *time*. We had started late, and after several hours we found our pace to have been on the average about 330 feet an hour. At our present rate, even supposing we could keep it up, we should be benighted still a considerable distance below the summit. The question therefore arose—at what hour must we turn back? With the idea of taking Morshead down to Camp IV before dark, we decided to turn at half past two. By that hour we had reached an elevation close upon 27,000 feet. Though the effort of moving upwards was increasingly difficult, we could breathe easily enough at rest, and we contentedly viewed the landscape as we sat on a ledge, eating chocolate, sugar and raisins.

For the judging mind outside the event it would have been easy to see that we were a defeated party some hours before, perhaps even so soon as we were compelled to camp no higher than 25,000 feet. Whether the summit of Mount Everest, had we attained it, would have aroused in us a quality of emotion worthy of the occasion is impossible to tell; but we experienced certainly nothing of the kind at this highest point we reached. The stupefied brain had remained only capable of turning aside from all else and concentrating on the one grim task of pushing upward. Relieved now of the necessity of attention to that, it could perceive one light for guidance, dimly but steadily burning: the training of a mountaineer, teaching him to know what dangers mean and to understand that it is a fool's game to ignore them, informed us now. We accepted the fact that we had failed to climb Mount Everest; we saw that, if ever we were to try again, we must cry halt and go no higher.

The descent to Camp IV was remarkably quick; at four o'clock we picked up Morshead and shortly afterwards were moving back along the sloping, broken ledges towards the crest of the ridge. The fresh snow rendered this an awkward passage and the party had long since lost the keen edge of their alertness. The third man slipped, carrying with him the second and fourth on the rope. Warned by unusual sounds behind him, the leader struck the pick of his axe into the snow and hitched the rope around it. He was able to press firmly on the shaft with one hand while holding the rope with the other. Nothing more could be done. It was a hundred to one that either the axe-head would be pulled out or the rope broken; the three bodies gathering momentum were in danger of slipping more than 3,000 feet before they could come to rest on a snowy plateau. After a few seconds, by a miracle as it seemed, they were strung out down the slope, with a sound rope tightly stretched between them, and then almost at once recovered their footing.

Less than two hours later, after toilsome step-cutting, we seemed to have met all our difficulties. But Morshead had come to the end of his tether; in his exhausted state he could come down only a few steps at a time. It had already been dark for an hour when we reached the North Col and it was half past eleven when we crawled at last into our tents.

The result of these experiences was apparent when we came down to the base camp. Morshead was severely frostbitten in toes and fingers; Norton's ear and my three finger-tips could not be entirely disregarded, and more serious was injury to both our hearts. Somervell alone remained fit enough to be counted on the strength of the climbing contingent.

A second attempt to reach the summit was made a few days later by Finch and Geoffrey Bruce. They used oxygen above 22,000 feet and found that, in spite of its weight, the apparatus helped them. They chose for their camp a rocky platform on the back of the ridge at 25,500 feet. In that exposed position they had to fight a gale of wind and spent most of the night in struggling with their tent. As the wind did not abate until the middle of the next day, they had to remain for a second night at this elevation. Oxygen helped them to keep warm but also increased their appetites. They continued next day, taking up with them Tejbir, one of our four Gurkha N.C.O.s. This man was to carry spare oxygen cylinders, a huge load of over 50 pounds, as far as he could, perhaps to 27,000 feet, and the other two would go on from there with fresh cylinders, leaving Tejbir where he was or sending him down. But Tejbir failed to get higher than 26,000 feet. Finch and Bruce wore themselves out with the effort of carrying spare cylinders beyond the full complement of four and finally abandoned them. They left the ridge on account of the prevailing wind, which was now blowing again, and at 27,235 feet were obliged to turn back, exhausted from want of food.

The facts of the third attempt may be put yet more briefly; for the climbers were still short of 23,000 feet when an avalanche came down upon them, overwhelming seven porters and carrying them over the tip of a huge crevasse to their death. Nothing more need to be said of that ill-fated going forth after the first snow of the monsoon had fallen.

How are we to think of the whole problem of climbing Mount Everest? Little doubt remains that our porters could carry our camp a stage higher, and with a camp at 27,000 feet we should have a good chance of reaching the summit with or without oxygen. But it must not be forgotten that to push our final camp a stage higher, still more to get the oxygen cylinders to that height, requires time and transport. In regard to the weather our experience so far has revealed a dilemma: if we escape the bitter northwest wind to which the ridge is exposed, we must expect a monsoon current threatening snow and even worse conditions for climbing. The weather will have to mend such bad habits if any party is going to have a fair chance of reaching the summit and getting down again. And we must not forget the descent; the party of the first attempt in 1922 are not likely to forget it. The descent after all is part of the game. No mountaineer would be content to reach the top and not get down. The climbing-party for 1924 will have the advantage of knowing at the start what their aim must be and they will almost certainly be equipped with a more efficient oxygen apparatus. They can hardly find fortune more ill-disposed than we did in 1922, and with it but a little more favourable, they should achieve the conquest of Mount Everest.   * * *

Published as 'Everest Unvanquished'

Asia Magazine, No. 9, 1923

9

THRONES IN HEAVEN
Mount Everest, 24 May 1924

'Accordingly a twofold operation was carried out on the 24th—the evacuation of Camp III and the rescue of the marooned men from Camp IV. Of this Mallory will tell the story. That he was himself suffering from the prevalent high-altitude cough—which prevents sleep at night and handicaps the climber— and yet was the mainspring of two fine climbs, he will probably not tell, but few would, or could, have done what he did.... Here I let Mallory take up the story.'

The Times despatch No 7 by Edward Norton, published on 16 June 1924.

This pause in our protracted struggle does not seem the moment for telling a story: Norton probably thinks so as he hands over this part of his task to me. Action is only suspended before the more intense action of the climax. The issue will shortly be decided. The third time we walk up East Rongbuk Glacier will be the last, for better or for worse. We have counted our wounded and know, roughly, how much to strike off the strength of our little army as we plan the next act of the battle.

In making plans, however, though we turn from the story of the past to the brighter future, we have been brought to consider certain events of the past few days. The events all belong to one stage—between Camp, 21,000 feet short of the summit. In 1922 the way here consisted of a brief hour's easy going up the stones of the glacier, followed by a steeper ascent of about 1,400 feet on snow and ice slopes, and up and down these slopes the men went freely, without thought of the difficulties, until the party of 17 was swept off them by an avalanche, and seven porters were killed. That was on 7 June, after the first big snowfall of the monsoon of 3-5 June. Naturally now in 1924 we do not mean to be caught in the same way again, not if we can help it.

It is when we think and think how we can make safe the way to Camp IV up on the snowy shelf among the great ice-cliff of Chang La that we begin to appreciate the immense difficulties Everest holds in store. It must be remembered, in the first place, that our great ally, the Sherpa porter, is not a practised mountaineer. Give him good, hard snow where nails can grip, slopes where he can just walk comfortably on good steps carved by the Sahib's ice-axe clean and clear, unencumbered by fresh powdery snow; give him a rope for a handrail here and there at danger points; give him above all, to believe that at the journey's end he will find good food and a warm bed, and he will go up and down steep tracks without a qualm, happy confident and safe.

But the mountain does not always acquiesce in this cheerful view. The first weapon of defence is simply the cold. It seems cold beyond a certain point somewhere about—10 deg. Fahrenheit at night. The cold at these altitudes and under these conditions of their life are considered, that the porters, with few exceptions, lose their vitality most quickly in great cold. Nor can it be said that the British Sahib is unaffected.

The second weapon is the snow. The fewest inches of snow enormously increase the labour of carrying a load from Camp III to Camp IV. All that was firm and sure becomes slippery and uncertain. The porter no longer distinguishes clearly the hole where his foot may be placed in the new snow, and is inclined to slide on the hard old snow or on the ice beneath as the powdery stuff blows up into his face. Instead of stepping in glad confidence, body erect, he begins hesitatingly to crawl, with his body hugging the slope. All sense of security is gone; the splendid fellow who bore his load so proudly has become a veritable child, a child for whom the British officer is at every turn responsible.

Irvine, Mallory, Norton, Odell, and The Times runner, rear. Shebbeare, Bruce, Somervell, Beetham, seated.

The fortune of this expedition in 1924 is sharply differentiated from our experiences in 1922 by the greater cold this year and the greater snowfall to date. It is, of course, the snowfall which has chiefly affected the mountaineering difficulties between Camps III and IV. The particular slope of the corridor where the avalanche occurred in 1922 is not dangerous every day, and was in perfectly good condition when Norton, Odell and myself set forth to reach Chang La on the 20th. Nevertheless, warnings of bad weather already received convinced us that we must establish at the outset a way independent of this slope in case of heavy snow.

The Rules of the Game

The rules of this game, so to speak, are that you may directly ascend a slope in comparative safety, but must never cross a slope where the snow is likely to slip just by crossing it, and so breaking the surface, you are likely to start an avalanche. The corridor in 1922 was unsafe after the monsoon snow had fallen because the floor was on a slant, so that though one might feel that one was going directly up a slope, one was really crossing one all the time. Now as one looks up at the intermingled masses of white broken snow and bluish broken ice below the long snow saddle called Chang La, or North Col, it is almost unimaginable, if one does not take the corridor leading directly to the strategical point, that it will be possible to regain this line without crossing one or other of the snow slopes, all of which are dangerous to cross after sufficient snowfall.

Away to the right, separated from the corridor by a series of ice-cliffs, we saw the long slopes used for the ascent by the first 1921 expedition. The place has changed a good deal since, but the lower slopes remain substantially as they were, while higher an immense crevasse curves across the face and stretches to the upper end of the corridor. Would it be possible to use this crevasse if we came up to the right to take us back to the heart of the corridor? Clearly, on the lower lip if we could work along, we should be protected from an avalanche from above. Any party making fresh tracks up to Chang La from Camp III will find they have a full day work's work, though on the 20th we had favourable conditions and went slowly enough. At length, the steep slope brought us in the crevasse and the one real difficulty of the route. On the lower lip, which we wanted to follow, impinged hereabouts a line of ice-cliffs. It was necessary to climb up the steep wall to the foot of the little chimney, which here presented our crevasse. The snow in the bed of this chimney gave no foothold; steps could not be cut in its sides, so inconveniently narrow it was. Before we emerged and found ourselves on the big crevasse proper, with the lip fortunately accessible, we had climbed 200 feet as steep and difficult as one could wish to find on any big mountain.

The rest of the way gave no trouble, though taking the straight way in order to avoid traversing the final slope up to the old site of Camp IV involved more step-cutting. We congratulated ourselves on having shared the labours of the day, so each could feel satisfied at his part and also at having eliminated the principal dangers on the way up. But it remained to be seen how the porters would manage the loads up that steep 200 feet.

On the following day, the 21st, Somervell, Irvine, and Hazard set forth to escort the first lot of loads to Camp IV. It was snowing slightly when they started and the day grew worse. Somervell found our tracks covered or could not find them at all. The ice chimney no doubt they rightly decided was too narrow for the majority of the loads. Somervell and Irvine established themselves at the top while Hazard directed operations from below and all twelve loads were hauled up. Tremendous efforts must have been required of those two who hauled and the two or three porters who helped. Two hours and a half were thus spent. Having seen Hazard up to the foot of the final slope Somervell and Irvine returned. According to plan the porters were to rest next day at Camp IV before going on with Bruce and Odell to establish Camp V. This operation has to be conducted with oxygen. Irvine was now wanted in camp to prepare the apparatus for the next day. In such thick weather Somervell judged that Irvine must have a companion on the descent.

An Anxious Night

A further illustration of the mountaineering difficulties in reaching Camp IV is the story of the party conducted by Bruce and Odell on the 23rd, a day later than they were due to go up. Fresh snow had greatly altered the easy walk up the stones of the glacier. Instead of a brief hour up to the foot of the slopes nearly three hours were required. On the slopes themselves snow was found to be in the most disagreeable state. Hazard was apparently deaf to their shoutings, and for an hour or so the two parties were never in touch.

The two stories we heard in Camp III that evening, with the news that not all Hazard's party had descended, mingled as we lay in our tents with the sound of ever-increasing snowfall, produced the nearest thing to gloom I remember during the expedition. As night came on, the snow had a moister and stickier quality. Was this really the monsoon then? Four men caught on Chang La for the first snow of the monsoon. One of them reported frost-bitten. It was this circumstance that compelled rescue the next day and no later. I woke in the early part of the night for a coughing fit. The tent was brighter, and Norton murmured: 'The moon.' Sure enough, looking behind me, I made out through the canvas a bright unclouded moon. The snow had stopped. It was not the monsoon this time.

Was there ever such a party as set out straggling up the snow-covered stones next morning? Norton, Somervell, and myself, the three who have climbed together on Everest before, must have appeared like a party of thrashed curs. I suppose we were half sick with the cold and the altitude. Never can three men have looked less like accomplishing a hard task; never, I confess, has a task appeared to me so utterly far away and unlikely to be accomplished. We drove ourselves somehow or other over the fresh snow of the glacier basin and up, up, slowly and wearily, puffing and coughing. 'If only it were not for that blessed cough,' I thought, 'even in snow up to my knees I could have gone on well enough.'

We started at 8 am; at 1:30 pm we were at the foot of the steep place below the ice chimney. Every ledge and step was filled with snow. But there remained the thin descending line of rope, fixed by Somervell's party to help the porters. That blessed rope! How pleased we were to grasp it with both hands and pull ourselves up the steep places! On two dangerous sections above the crevasse Norton and Somervell in turn went ahead on the long rope, while the remaining two secured them.

While Somervell was leading up and across the final slope, the four porters above were held in conversation. As there was no time to lose, we wanted to know whether all were ready to move. The question appeared to puzzle them. Eventually one asked, 'Up or down?' Norton's reply seemed to surprise no less than delight them, so little had they realised the situation or, appreciated the threat of more bad weather. It was 4.30 p.m., and we were already in cold shadow when Somervell reached the shelf, or, rather, reached within a few feet of it, for the rope on which we held him was just too short for the purpose. The quickest way, we had decided, was to make a handrail and send down the men one at a time to where Norton, and I were posted; but now the proposed handrail did not reach far enough, and the men had to move two or three steps before they could reach it.

Watching with some anxiety, Norton and I suddenly saw two of the four men sliding down the steep snow slope. By some miracle they stopped some 15ft below. Somervell was entirely equal to the occasion. We heard him shout 'What's khaskura for "Stay still"?' Norton gave the right expression, and the two, clinging in their precarious situation with fingers dug into the snow—neither had an ice-axe—were duly instructed not to stir for their lives. The others were passed along the rope. Somervell stuck his ice-axe into the snow and passed a rope round it and in a few minutes we saw him apparently gather to his bosom the errant porters, in a paternal manner worthy of Abraham. The two were passed along the rope.

It had been our great good fortune to find that the frost-bitten member of the party of porters had suffered not in his feet but in his hands. We had not to use our one man-carrier brought up by Norton. He could go down on his own feet. He was a very sick man nevertheless. The ice chimney was no place for one hardly able to bear holding the fixed rope and in our race with the oncoming darkness, he necessarily suffered. But it was well for him, as for us, that the race was ours.

As I headed the party, trudging a little grimly across the glacier basin in the last light of day, I dimly made out a party approaching. It was Noel and Odell, with two or three porters bearing hot soup in thermos flasks. *Sic itur ad astra.* They will deserve their thrones in Heaven. But not every party descending from Chang La will find good tracks and an untroubled evening, still less will they meet hot soup. We know now what we have to do to make safe the way. Yet perhaps it will be as well he should not deign to take much notice of the little group of busy ones on the great North side, or, at all events, that he should not observe among the scattered remnants he has half put to flight the still existent will, perhaps power, to singe his very nose tip.

* * *

Published as the 7th Mount Everest Despatch

The Times, May 24 1924.

Camp VI 26,700 about here. Norton and Somervell about here 28,130, June 4. Mallory and Irvine last seen about here 28,230 June 8.

Mallory and Irvine set off for the Summit of Mount Everest on 4 June 1924.

Mallory's body was retrieved on 1 May 1999.

NOTES

1 Published in 1920 as the article went to press.

2 *Österreichische Allgemeine Zeitung* 1889.

3 *Boll. C.A.I.,* 268-80.

4 I use this expression to denote, not a state of intermittent vomiting, but simply one in which physical exertion exhausts the body abnormally, and causes a remarkable disinclination to further exertion.

5 Nevertheless, I think it a wise precaution to avoid much sleeping at camps as high as 20,000 feet.

6 It had not yet been established that the true direction of this arête is North-east.

7 The coolies had been divided into three parties which were to spend four or five days in the advanced camp by turns to be trained in the practice of mountaineering while the rest supplied this camp from our base.

8 Calculated from the readings of two aneroids, allowing a correction for the height of the camp as established later by Major Wheeler.

9 The survey established the height of this peak as 22,520 feet, and our subsequent experience suggests that aneroid barometers habitually read too high when approaching the

upper limit of their record.

10 In the Rongbuk Valley there was no wood and our supply of yak dung had to come up from Chöbuk.

11 A useful coolie with experience in the Indian Army. I had used him as second Sirdar.

12 It turned out to be a full 1,200 feet.

13 [Repetition:] *The whole plan of campaign had been founded upon the belief that September would be the best month for climbing, and our greatest efforts, some sort of an assault upon the mountain, were timed to take place then. We must now proceed upon the assumption that what the wise men prophesied about the matter would come true; and they promised a fine September.*

14 [Repetition:] *The first object which our plans must include was, of course, to reach Chang La; by finding the way to this point we should establish a line of attack and complete a stage of our reconnaissance. Secondly we must aim at reaching the North-east Shoulder. In so far as it was an object of reconnaissance to determine whether it was possible to climb Mount Everest, our task could never be complete until we had actually climbed it; but short of that it was important to have a view of the final stage and, could we reach the great shoulder of the arête, we should at least be in a better position to estimate what lay between there and the summit. Finally we saw no reason to exclude the supreme object itself. It would involve no sacrifice of meaner ends; the best would not interfere with the good. For if it should turn out that the additional supplies required for a longer campaign were more than our coolies could carry, we would simply drop them and aim less high.*

In organising the assault we had first to consider how our camps could be established, at Lhakpa La or perhaps better beyond it at a lower elevation, at Chang La, and finally as high as possible, somewhere under the shoulder, we thought, at about 26,500 feet. From the camp on Chang La we should have to carry up ten loads, each of 15 lb., which would provide tents enough, and sleeping-sacks and food for a maximum of four Sahibs and four coolies; sixteen coolies were allowed for this task; twelve therefore would have to return on the day of their ascent and sleep at Chang La, and on the assumption that they would require an escort of Sahibs who must also sleep at this camp, four small tents must remain there, making six in all to be carried up to this point. The lower end of the ladder must be so constructed as to support this weight at the top.

15 *[Repetition:] I had hoped we should have a full complement of coolies on the 22nd, but when morning came it was found that three, including two of the best men, were too ill to start. Consequently some of the loads were rather heavier than I intended. But all arrived safely at Lhakpa La before midday. Visited by malicious gusts from the North-west, the pass was cheerless and chilly; however, the rim afforded us some protection, and we decided to pitch our tents there rather than descend on the other side with the whole party, a move which I felt might complicate the return. I was not very happy about the prospects for the morrow. For my own part I had been excessively and unaccountably tired in coming up to the col; I observed no great sparkle of energy or enthusiasm among my companions; Sanglu was practically hors de combat, some of the coolies had with difficulty been brought to the col and were more or less exhausted; and many complaints of headache, even from the best of them, were a bad sign.*

There was no question of bustling off before dawn on the 23rd, but we rose early enough, as I supposed, to push on to Chang La if we were sufficiently strong. Morshead and I in a Mummery tent had slept well and I congratulated myself on an act of mutilation in cutting two large slits in its roof. The rest had not fared so well, but seemed fit enough, and the wonderful prospect from our camp at sunrise was a cheering sight. With the coolies, however, the case was different. Those who had been unwell overnight had not recovered, and it was evident that only a comparatively small number would be able to come on; eventually I gathered ten, two men who both protested they were ill casting lots for the last place; and of these ten it was evident that none was unaffected by the height and several were more seriously mountain-sick. Under these circumstances it was necessary to consider which loads should be carried on, Bury, Wollaston and Morshead suggested that they should go back at once so as not to burden the party with the extra weight of their belongings, and it seemed the wisest plan that they should return. Certain stores were left behind at Lhakpa La as reserve supplies for the climbing party. I decided at an early hour that our best chance was to take an easy day; after a late start and a very slow march we pitched our tents on the open snow up towards the col.

It might have been supposed that in so deep a cwm and sheltered on three sides by steep mountain slopes, we should find a tranquil air and the sooth-ing, though chilly calm of undisturbed frost. Night came clearly indeed, but with no gentle intentions. Fierce squalls of wind visited our tents and shook and worried them with the disagreeable threat of tearing them away from their moorings, and then scurried off, leaving us in wonder at the change and asking what next to expect. It was a cold wind at an altitude of 22,000 feet, and however little one may have suffered, the atmosphere discouraged sleep. Again I believe I was more fortunate than my companions, but Bullock and Wheeler fared badly. It was an hour or so after sunrise when we left the camp and half an hour later we were breaking the crust on the first slopes under the wall. We had taken three coolies who were sufficiently fit and competent, and now proceeded to use them for the hardest work. Apart from one brief spell of cutting when we passed the corner of a bergschrund it was a matter of straightforward plugging, firstly slanting up to the right on partially frozen avalanche snow and then left in one long upward traverse to the summit. Only one passage shortly below the col caused either anxiety or trouble; here the snow was lying at a very steep angle and was deep enough to be disagreeable. About 500 steps of very hard work cov-ered all the worst of the traverse and we were on the col shortly before 11.30 a.m. By this time two coolies were distinctly tired, though by no means inca-pable of coming on; the third, who had been in front, was comparatively fresh. Wheeler thought he might be good for some further effort, but had lost all feeling in his feet. Bullock was tired, but by sheer will power would evi-dently come on—how far, one couldn't say. For my part I had had the won-derful good fortune of sleeping tolerably well at both high camps and now finding my best form; I supposed I might be capable of another 2,000 feet, and there would be no time for more. But what lay ahead of us? My eyes had often strayed, as we came up, to the rounded edge above the col and the final rocks below the North-east arête. If ever we had doubted whether the arête were accessible, it was impossible to doubt any longer. For a long way up those easy rock and snow slopes was neither danger nor difficulty. But at present there was wind. Even where we stood under the lee of a little ice cliff it came in fierce gusts at frequent intervals, blowing up the powdery snow in a suffocating tourbillon.

16 [Repetition:] *It remained to take a final decision on the morning of the 25th. We were evidently too weak a party to play a waiting game at this altitude. We must either take our camp to the col or go back. A serious objection to going forward lay in the shortage of coolies' rations. Had the men been fit it would not have been too much for them to return, as I had planned, unladen to Lhakpa La and reach Chang La again the same day. I doubted whether any two could be found to do that now; and to subtract two was to leave only eight, of whom two were unfit to go on, so that six would remain to carry seven loads. However, the distance to the col was so short that I was confident such difficulties could be overcome one way or another. A more unpleasant consideration was the thought of requiring a party which already felt the height too much to sleep at least a 1,000 feet higher. We might well find it more than we could do to get back over Lhakpa La, and be forced to make a hungry descent down the Rongbuk Valley. There would be no disaster in that event. The crucial matter was the condition of the climbers. Were we fit to push the adventure further? The situation, if any one of the whole party collapsed, would be extremely disagreeable, and all the worse if he should be one of the Sahibs, who were none too many to look after the coolies in case of mountaineering difficulties. Such a collapse I judged might well be the fate of one or other of us if we were to push our assault along Chang La to the limit of our strength. And what more were we likely to accomplish from a camp on Chang La? The second night had been no less windy than the first. Soon after the weather cleared the wind had been strong from the North-west, and seemed each day to become more violent. The only signs of a change now pointed to no improvement, but rather to a heavy fall of snow—by no means an improbable event according to local lore. The arguments, in fact, were all on one side;*

it would be bad heroics to take wrong risks; and fairly facing the situation one could only admit the necessity of retreat.

It may be added that the real weakness of the party became only too apparent in the course of the return journey over Lhakpa La on this final day; and it must be safe to say that none of the three climbers has ever felt a spasm of regret about the decision to go back or a moment's doubt as to its rightness. It was imposed upon us by circumstances without a reasonable alternative.

[17] See *Geographical Journal*.

[18] [Repetition:] *On 20 May sunlight hit the tents at 5 a.m. according to our time. I immediately got up to rouse the party. There was no sign of life in the porters' tents, which were hermetically sealed. Muffled responses from the interior carried no conviction of minds alert and eager. It was necessary to untie the elaborate fastenings by which the flaps were secured. The porters, I found, were all unwell—we eventually ascertained that four of them were seriously mountain-sick. Five were willing to come on. It was hardly surprising that they felt better when they were persuaded to come out of the unventilated tents.*

[19] Since writing this we have the figures worked out by Morshead from theodolite observations at Base Camp; according to them we reached 29,985; but we cannot deduce from this the exact rise on the final day since Camp V is unfixed by theodolite.